THE SELF-PUBLISHING WORKBOOK

"Julie Postance is a book angel sent from above! She changed the way I see myself and what I believe to be possible, and for that I am forever grateful. Julie empowered me to tell my story, my authentic way. *Opshopulence* became #1 on Amazon in Fashion and Textiles and stayed there for weeks. A sold-out launch in New York at Refashion Week followed shortly after, as did a live TV cross from NYC to Studio 10 in Sydney, Australia, to promote my book. Recently, one of my Thrift Tip TikToks went viral and I ended up in *The Sun* newspaper in the UK! It's amazing to see what happens with passion and the right team to guide you. Working with Julie and her team was an incredible experience—life-changing, actually! If you want to write a book, Julie Postance and her stable of literary angels are like no other."

—Faye De Lanty, author of *Opshopulence*

"I'm so grateful to Julie Postance. With her support, I've now published three bestselling books on Aware Parenting. My most recent book, *I'm Here and I'm Listening* has been #1 in four categories; my second, *The Emotional Life of Babies* has been #1 in six categories; and my first, which I coauthored with Lael Stone, *Raising Compassionate and Resilient Children* was #1 in nine categories including Motherhood, Parenting and Family, Movers and Shakers, Developmental Child Psychology and Bestsellers, and Hot New Releases. This has been a dream come true. I'm now planning to launch four more!"

—Marion Rose, PhD, author of *Raising Compassionate and Resilient Children*

"Holding my first book is one of the proudest personal achievements in my life. That's a great motivator by itself. My first children's book, *My Strong Mind,* became successful with translations in eleven languages and a decent extra income selling online in the US, UK, Canada, and Australia. I then went on to create two more children's books in my *Positive Mindset* series and another book entitled *How I Beat My Bully*. I sold 25,000 books across all channels, making $140K in royalties for four children's books in a year. Online publishing is less risky and more scalable than printing your own books. I always liked Julie's hands-on approach. We worked hard and got stuff done, learning while being in good company! Once you know how to self-publish, you can do it for the rest of your life. The value of the coaching stays. I now sell 60 books a day."

—Niels van Hove, author of the *Social Skills & Mental Health for Kids* series and the *Positive Mindset* series

"I created and launched my beautiful children's book, *Jo-Jo the Kind Sloth: A Children's Book about Self-Compassion,* during the Children's Book Empire program. With the mentorship and guidance of Julie Postance every step of the way, not only did I achieve a lifelong dream of creating a children's book, but I also cocreated it with my son, Joseph, and hit #1 in two Amazon categories in less than 24 hours! It was #1 in Children's Books on Emotions & Feelings and #1 in Children's Books on Values. It's been selling well on Amazon; I'm now creating more books and have just done a TEDx talk about self-compassion. I highly recommend Julie Postance and her company for the high touch, support, and encouragement!"

—Dr. Olivia Ong, The Heart-Centred Doctor and award-winning, best-selling author

"I can't praise Julie highly enough. She's not only a master of her craft but incredibly generous with her insights and desire to share the benefits of her experience. Most importantly, Julie genuinely cares about her clients and wants them to be successful."

—Kate Christiansen, author of *The Thrive Cycle* and Director of The Adaptive Advantage

"Julie's guidance proved invaluable and helped me indie publish a book of an exceptional professional standard. My book has done so well. I sold 4,000 copies in one month through my website and now I have made a deal with a major Australian publisher. Thank you for your help, Julie. I couldn't have done it without you!"

—Shannon Kelly White, author of *Shannon's Kitchen*

"With Julie's guidance, I self-published a small book called *Survive FBT: Skills Manual for Parents Undertaking Family Based Treatment (FBT) for Child and Adolescent Anorexia Nervosa*, which has sold thousands of copies and helped people all over the globe. As a result of its success, it has been picked up by Japanese, Swedish, and Norwegian publishers. I've also self-published it in German and Italian. I then went on to cowrite and self-publish two other books, *Unpack Your Eating Disorder: The Journey to Recovery for Adolescents in Treatment, and Letting Go of ED—Embracing Me: A Journal of Self-Discovery*, as well as produce a deck of therapeutic cards for sufferers of eating disorders. Not only have I become a renowned global expert in my field, but I feel I have made a difference to thousands of sufferers of eating disorders from around the world."

—Maria Ganci, author of *Survive FBT, Unpack Your Eating Disorder* and *Letting Go of ED* and Registered Clinical Mental Health Social Worker and Child and Adolescent Psychoanalytical Psychotherapist.

"Julie was recommended to me by a colleague who had successfully used Julie's guidance to publish her own picture book. Julie didn't disappoint. My children's book, *No Matter What*, not only became #1 on Amazon in six categories, which included Children's Books Emotions and Feelings, Children's Books Growing Up & The Fact of Life, Children's Books on Adoption, Children's Books on Values, Children's Books on Parents, but what is even more incredible is it also became #1 in the entire Amazon.com.au bookstore! I couldn't be happier with the result. I highly recommend Julie and Sophie for their publishing and marketing wisdom and expertise when it comes to getting a quality book and making it successful. I look forward to working with Julie again in the future."

—Dr. Kristen Crowhurst, author of *No Matter What*

"Thanks for all your help! *Yoga and the Alexander Technique* did well, and it has now been taken up by an American publisher who renamed it *Smart Yoga*. They have just negotiated rights with a Chinese and a Korean publisher to have the book translated, which is great. It has certainly raised my profile as an international presenter and teacher in this area."

—David Moore, author of *Smart Yoga*

"Since Julie took over the republishing of *Nine Days in Heaven* in March 2020, we have been selling about 4,000 copies per year. And our *Twelve Carols of Christmas* book, which commenced in November 2020, sold about 700 the first year and 1,100 the second year. We have been very happy with that."

—Dennis and Noelene Prince, authors of *Nine Days in Heaven* and *Twelve Carols of Christmas*

"I'd like to thank you and your team for all your outstanding work and efforts to publish my books, *The Betrayal Trauma Healing Workbook* and *The Pain and Betrayal Trauma Caused By Sexual Addiction* and getting them to #1 bestsellers. Thank you for all your ongoing support, validation, and understanding that I needed through this stressful and anxiety-inducing process. I'm really appreciative of all your amazing work. You're a great team, and I look forward to bringing more projects and clients to you."

—Dr. Fai Seyed, PhD, House of Hope Counselling and Psychotherapy Centre

"Thank you for your help with my book. It's out and getting a lot of traction. It's number two in Architectural Criticism in Australia. My primary goal for the book was to use it to find a good job, and I am being contacted on LinkedIn with good job offers! It has moved me from unknown in my field to the center."

—Chris Elliot, author of *The Great Landmark Race* and *Urban Designer*

"This has enabled me to fulfill a lifetime dream. I feel more confident and grounded in the direction the next part of my career will take. I feel happier working in a field I'd only ever dreamt about. My soul is content and grateful. The most exciting moment for me was when I received the first proof of my book. It was the first time I felt like a real author. I'd finally done it. Julie genuinely wants her clients to fulfill their desires and achieve the best possible outcomes. My favorite part of the process has been the tangible books I've held when my book arrives in the post as a proof, to smell the paper, read the story and have a real book in my hand. It's hard to talk about it without getting emotional. Doing this was the best risk I ever took. I have now published my second book and am working on three more. I've learned so much about the publishing process. I now feel confident to create more books and call myself an author. I'm thrilled that I followed my passion and dreams and took the risk to write."

—Stella Stamatakis, author of *What's a Yiayia?* and *Poppy Picker*

"I now have self-published six books and have been approached by a mainstream publisher to submit one—working on that at the moment!"

—Lisé Francis, author of the *My Awesome Family* series

"Since I launched my self-published memoir *Amelia & Me*, so many wonderful things have happened. The response has been beyond my wildest dreams. So far, I have been interviewed on Channel 7's *The Daily Edition*, *ABC Conversations*, Mia Freedman's *No Filter* podcast, The Queen Sesh with Constance Hall and Annaliese and the Kinderling *Kids Radio Conversations* program. Book-related extracts and articles have been promoted by Mamamia, Kidspot, the Deafness Forum of Australia, BubHub, Australian Hearing, Amaze and so on. There's also been news coverage at the local (*The Star Weekly*) and national level (feature in Books section of the *The Weekend Australian* and a story on the *9Honey News* website). My book journey has taken me to cities including Sydney and Brisbane to meet brilliant women such as Sarah Kanowski, Mia Freedman, and Shevonne Hunt. It has also connected me with so many families who have related to my story and reached out to share their personal experiences with me. The response has been so touching as countless parents have written to tell me that they see themselves in the pages of my book and as a result feel less alone. I could not have achieved any of this without the guidance, expertise and vision of Julie Postance. She is an inspiration to me."

—Melinda Hildebrandt, author of *Amelia & Me: On Deafness, Autism and Parenting by the Seat of My Pants*

"I was feeling frustrated at so many years of never getting close to publishers. I wanted to achieve my goal of publishing books as I knew I could write well but didn't know what to do with my two finished manuscripts. My *Baby Days* book was added to the *Victorian Baby Bundle*, which will mean at least 50,000 babies (yes, you read that correctly!) will be reading my book, which is pretty special. *A Grain of Hope* led to speaking gigs at schools and a launch with the renowned barrister and human rights advocate Julian Burnside. I feel like I've birthed two books that now have their own place in children's lives."

—Nicola Philps, teacher and author of *Baby Days* and *A Grain of Hope*

"I wrote my book to help women have more energy and to share how I have gone from being an exhausted working mom on autopilot, to now being full of energy and living consciously on my terms. Thanks to Julie, my book has now been sold globally, my book has helped establish my credibility in the spiritual wellness space, and I have been able to build my online communities in the thousands. I absolutely loved working with Julie. I had never self-published a book, and it was wonderful to have Julie's expertise guiding me through the whole process. Julie made the whole process seamless. I am so, so grateful for Julie's skillful coaching through the process and forever grateful that she helped me bring my book to life. I highly recommend Julie to anyone wanting to publish their book."

—Alicia Dumais Temmerman, lawyer, business owner and author of *Pure Energy*

"It was a dream come true. Never in my wildest dreams did I feel I would have had all the opportunities pop up for me, such as TV, podcasts, blogs, and magazines. I also feel so happy when I hear parents and kids tell me the book exactly describes their child. I love hearing feedback about how children have started to learn to self-regulate and find strategies to help them calm."

—Michelle Karavas, child and adolescent psychologist and author of *The Day My Brain Went Crazy*

"This book not only helps you develop and share your authentic voice with the world, but offers you expertise that only many years of experience in the self-publishing industry can bring. Julie has woven her magic through these pages and created easy-to-follow steps to help you on that seemingly overwhelming journey to becoming an author."

—Virginia Warren, lawyer and author of *Not Guilty* and *Let's Kiss All the Lawyers*

"Julie Postance's expertise and love for her subject shine through in *The Self-Publishing Workbook* and *The Book Inside You Journal*. If you want to know how to start, finish, publish, and market your book, this is the guide for you!"
—Kate Olivieri, consultant

"Julie Postance is an absolute angel who can get you through the publishing creek without a paddle. Forever in gratitude!"
—Belinda Bailey, consultant and author of *The Love Codes*

"Julie is truly a master of her craft. I'm so excited to be able to share this with my clients and show them just how easy it really is to achieve their dream of becoming an author."
—Peta Webb, Owner *Crysalis Media*

"My book, *The Answers Are Within: A Life-Changing, Practical Guide to Trusting Your Intuition, and Finding Peace and Joy in Challenging Times* has just got the coveted #1 Bestseller Badge on Amazon in the Self-Esteem Self-Help category, outranking Brene Brown and Martha Beck! Special thanks and appreciation to Julie for holding my hand on this book publishing journey. Julie's wide experience and heart-centred approach along with her own published books made this a very rewarding experience."
—Anne Poole, author of *The Answers Are Within*

Published in Australia by
iinspire media
Melbourne, Australia
info@iinspiremedia.com.au
www.iinspiremedia.com.au

First published in Australia 2024

National Library of Australia Cataloguing in Publication entry

A catalogue record for this book is available from the National Library of Australia

Postance, Julie

The Self-Publishing Workbook: The Life-Changing Guide to Writing, Publishing, and Marketing Your Book, Becoming a Bestselling Author, and Making an Impact

ISBN: 978-0-9805953-4-5 (paperback)
ISBN: 978-0-9805953-5-2 (hardback)
ISBN: 978-0-9805953-6-9 (e-book)

Edited for US publication by Cortni L. Merritt
Cover design by Aleaca
Layout by Sophie White Design
Printed by IngramSpark

All care has been taken in the preparation of the information herein, but no responsibility can be accepted by the publisher or author for errors, omissions, or contrary interpretations on the subject matter. All details given in this book were current at the time of publication but are subject to change.

This book is for informational purposes only. The advice given in this book is based on the experience of the author. No guarantees for earnings or any other results of any kind are being made by the author or publisher, nor are any liabilities being assumed. The reader is entirely responsible for his or her actions. The author and publisher shall not be responsible for any person with regard to any loss or damage caused directly or indirectly by the information in this book. Professionals should be consulted for individual issues.

This book uses US English rather than Australian English and has been edited according to the US *Chicago Manual of Style*, 17th edition, to reach a wider audience.

Affiliate disclosure: Resources marked with an * are affiliate products, meaning the author receives a referral fee if the referral link is clicked and a purchase made at no extra expense to the purchaser. The author only recommends products and services that she has found to be the best in the field and she uses herself. Reader or purchaser are advised to do their own research before making any purchase online. No guarantee of earnings or other results of any kind nor any liability is assumed by the publisher or author.

iinspire media acknowledges the Wurundjeri Willum Clan and Taungurung People as the Traditional Owners and Custodians of the land on which we live and create. We recognize their living cultures and ongoing connection to Country and pay respect to their Elders past, present, and emerging.

The Self-Publishing Workbook

WORKBOOK

THE LIFE-CHANGING GUIDE
TO WRITING, PUBLISHING,
AND MARKETING YOUR BOOK,
BECOMING A BESTSELLING
AUTHOR, AND MAKING AN IMPACT

Julie Postance

THIS WORKBOOK BELONGS TO

_____

_____

If found, please return to

Address
_____

City
_____

Mobile
_____

Email
_____

Instagram
_____

Facebook
_____

Website
_____

To download my Self-Publishing Checklist
and Book Template, please go to

WWW.IINSPIREMEDIA.COM.AU

ABOUT THE AUTHOR

Julie Postance is a leading self-publishing consultant and the director of *iinspire media*, a company that has helped hundreds of people fulfill their dreams of becoming successful published authors.

She has an excellent track record of making her clients #1 bestsellers on Amazon.

Julie works individually and in groups with a diverse range of people, including CEOs, doctors, entrepreneurs, lawyers, therapists, teachers, counselors, and stay-at-home parents.

As a speaker, teacher, and consultant, Julie guides her students, clients, and audiences to find their authentic voice and own their visibility through publishing a high-quality book that makes an impact in the world.

Julie is a self-published author and ghostwriter of six books on subjects ranging from self-publishing, hearing loss, health and fitness, baby sign language, cosmology, and dating—all of which have made a difference to the readers they serve.

Julie has over 20 years' experience as a publishing, communications, and marketing consultant in writing, editing, publishing, ghostwriting, and marketing. Julie's clients include: Aurora School, The Victorian Deaf Education Institute, The Department of Education and Early Childhood Development, The Ethics Centre NSW, Deaf Children Australia, Australian Stem Cell Healthcare, Hay House Australia, Guide Dogs Victoria, International Guide Dogs Federation, Mills Oakley Lawyers, Hear for You Australia, The Melbourne City Living Guide, On the Go Tours London, Matchmedia (UK), and View London (UK).

She is the proud mum of miracle twin boys, Ollie and Arie, and fur baby Pud. They live in Melbourne, Australia.

WARNING

THIS WORKBOOK
WILL CHANGE
YOUR LIFE.

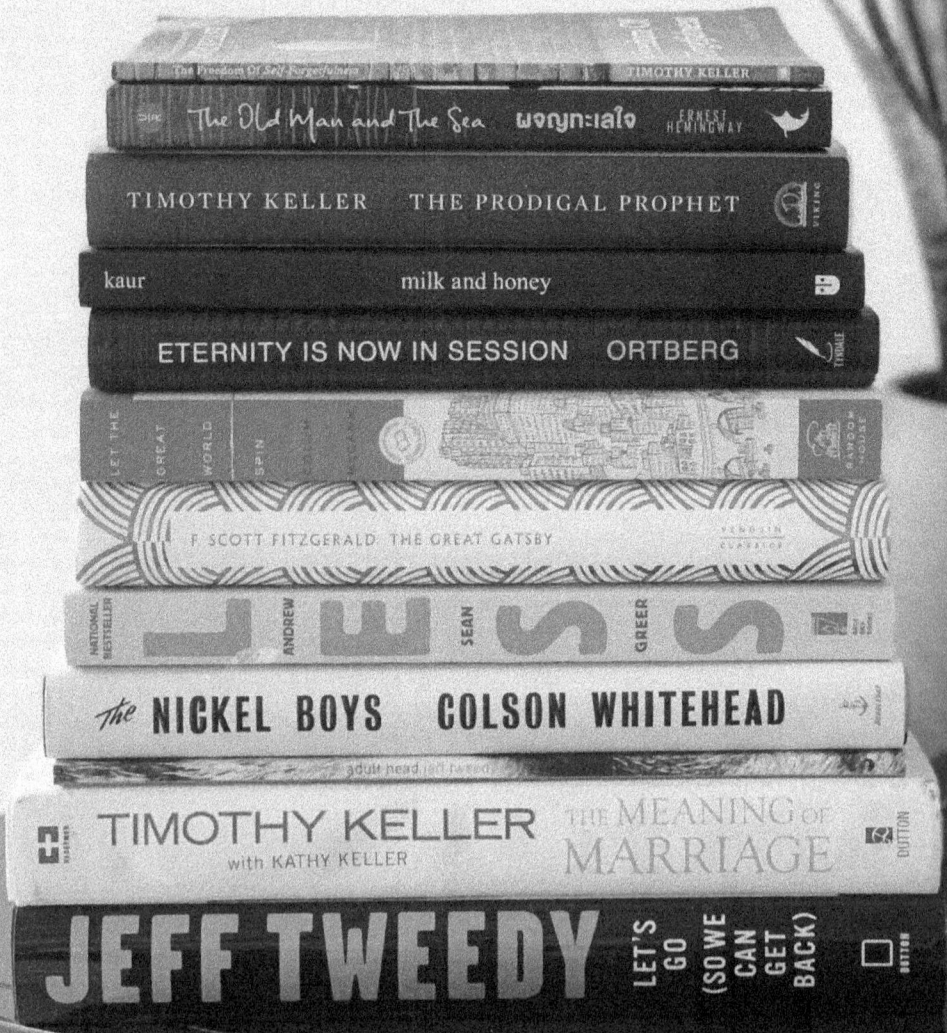

The Freedom Of Self Forgetfulness — TIMOTHY KELLER

The Old Man and The Sea — ชายชราและทะเล — ERNEST HEMINGWAY

TIMOTHY KELLER — THE PRODIGAL PROPHET

kaur — milk and honey

ETERNITY IS NOW IN SESSION — ORTBERG

LET THE GREAT WORLD SPIN

F. SCOTT FITZGERALD THE GREAT GATSBY

LESS — NATIONAL BESTSELLER — ANDREW SEAN GREER

THE NICKEL BOYS — COLSON WHITEHEAD

TIMOTHY KELLER with KATHY KELLER — THE MEANING OF MARRIAGE

JEFF TWEEDY — LET'S GO (SO WE CAN GET BACK)

"I want to do something splendid... Something heroic or wonderful that won't be forgotten after I'm dead...I think I shall write books."

—Louisa May Alcott

Contents

"The power of a book lies in its power to turn a solitary act into a shared vision."

—Laura Bush, author of *Spoken from the Heart*

Introduction

Congratulations on taking this important step to becoming a published author. Launching a book into the world is one of the most rewarding experiences of your lifetime. With it, you get to leave a lasting legacy. You get to turn your unique story, wisdom, and your mastered craft into a tangible work of beautiful art that impacts the lives of others. You get to fulfill that lifelong dream of becoming a published author, holding your high-quality book in print that is produced as a paperback, hardback, e-book, and audiobook and made available across bookstores around the globe. You get to bring your talents, gifts, and strengths to something greater than yourself and make a difference on this planet.

As a published author, you become a "voice for the voiceless" as you bring your message to the audience you wish to serve. Your truth is communicated to your readership, forming a connection with them on a deep level and positively changing lives. You get to feel the satisfying sense of bliss of having fulfilled a purposeful endeavor. You can become a recognized authority or advocate in your field and generate a consistent passive income from ongoing book sales as your global exposure and credibility increases. There are countless benefits on this journey; however, it may be as simple as savoring that one definable moment—that indescribable feeling you get from holding your own published book in your hand, imbued with meaning and memories. It's a moment like no other.

So many of us feel called to tell that tale, share our message, write that memoir, educate, and enlighten. Yet many authors trip up at the point of publication, and manuscripts remain forgotten in one of the many folders on their desktop. Advances in the publishing industry have enabled writers to turn words into finished books in a far shorter time frame than if they were to go down the traditional publishing route and struggle for years to be accepted by a mainstream publishing company.

Traditional publishing is when you submit your manuscript to a mainstream publisher, and once accepted, they manage the production and distribution of your book. The publisher might pay you a small advance, and later, a small percentage of royalties. With self-publishing, on the other hand, you retain full creative control and make an upfront investment to an editor, cover designer, and book formatter to help produce your book, which you then publish yourself. Whether you choose traditional publishing or self-publishing, you still need to market the book yourself, or pay someone to do it for you. There is so much more creative freedom, speed to market, higher royalties, and earlier opportunities with self-publishing. But authors are frustrated because of the competing self-publishing options that come without a clear road map of what the process actually entails.

I'm Julie Postance, a self-publishing consultant who has helped hundreds of writers become successful authors, as well as being an independent author and ghostwriter of six nonfiction books. I'm also a firm believer that dying with the music inside you is no different than dying with an untold story tucked away in your top drawer.

That *book inside you*? I'm here to help you bring it into existence, nurture the seed until it's ready for the world, and from there, reap and grow from the benefits. Every day, I help writers achieve their independent publishing goals. I'm in the business of supporting people to take control of their writing careers and ensure their books bring the creative fulfillment they desire—whether turning their intellectual property into a long-term, income-generating asset; writing, publishing, and marketing a book that advances their career; creating an impressive, high-quality narrative that will be cherished by readers for having opened their hearts; or forging a money-making must-have in a specialized field that achieves meaningful and perhaps even groundbreaking results—I've seen it all.

WHY I CREATED THIS WORKBOOK

After walking beside so many on the self-publishing path, I felt compelled to capture in a workbook the exact process I use to guide my clients to highly successful book launches and ongoing authorship success. It contains the exact steps I teach my clients on how to write, publish, promote, become a #1 bestseller on Amazon, and sell a book successfully across global retailers. It walks you through step-by-step on how to produce your book as a paperback, hardback, and e-book, and then take it to market with confidence and a strategic plan.

Many of my clients who have applied my strategies have experienced huge wins in their creative and professional endeavors. For instance:

- Niels sold 25,000 children's books in his *Positive Mindset* series, had translations into 11 languages, and made $140K in royalties in one year.

- Marion and Lael's book *Raising Compassionate and Resilient Children* became #1 in nine categories on Amazon, and they were approached by the top two mainstream publishers to take over the distribution of their nonfiction book.

- Faye's book *Opshopulence* stayed #1 on Amazon in Fashion and Textiles for weeks and had a sold-out launch in New York.

- Shannon sold 4,000 copies of *Shannon's Kitchen* in her first month and was quickly picked up by a major publisher.

- Maria's book *Survive FBT* has sold thousands of copies and has been translated into four languages, positioning Maria as a renowned global expert in her field and making a difference to thousands of sufferers of eating disorders around the world.

- Nicola's book *Baby Days* was added to the *Victorian Baby Bundle*, which meant that at least 50,000 babies (yes, you read that correctly!) read her book.

Each of these people was a first-time author, brand new to the world of self-publishing, and shared the same fear and imposter syndrome experienced by most of us who embark on this path for the first time. If they can do it, trust me, you can too.

WHY SELF-PUBLISH?

Here are my top ten reasons why I'd recommend self-publishing over trying to get your manuscript published by a traditional or mainstream publisher:

1. Your chance of being published by a mainstream publisher is about 1%–2% (Talbot 2023).

2. If you get accepted by a mainstream publisher, the average time from acceptance by a mainstream publisher to bookshelf sales is 18 months.

3. Self-publishing sidesteps rejection letters and blows to your self-esteem. Instead, you can focus on building your author platform from the get-go.

4. You will bypass mainstream publishers and share your brilliance with the world, gain credibility, and earn money from your writing straight away.

5. More profit in your pocket. With a mainstream publisher, royalties average 6%–10% of net receipts. When you sell directly to your audience from your website or at events, you keep 100%. If you sell on Amazon, you'll earn between 35 and 70%. If you sell through a distributor, you'll get to keep 31.5%.

6. You have full control over your words, cover design, formatting, pricing—everything! You retain all rights to your book and oversee the entire publishing process. Updates can be made

over time to improve the book, so it evolves with you and your vision.

7. There's a whole world of creative professionals available online to collaborate with you! Editors, ghostwriters, cover designers, typesetters, and e-book converters, as well as publishing, printing, and distribution platforms, are just a Google search away, ready and willing to help produce your book.

8. Due to technological advances, self-publishing achieves the same high-quality printing and book distribution once reserved for traditionally published authors.

9. Print-on-demand (POD) ensures affordability for the author and sustainability for the environment. You can print one or 1,000 books, depending on your plans for distribution.

10. Your chances of engagement with a mainstream publisher are greater with a self-published book to your name. Richard Paul Evans took six weeks to write the 87-page *The Christmas Box*. He self-published it, sold it to family and friends, and then watched it soar. Mainstream publishing house Simon & Schuster caught wind of his success and paid him $4.2 million for it!

The Self-Publishing Workbook is a content-rich, interactive, motivational guidebook designed to step you through the writing and independent publishing journey, so the foundations of your book *and* its marketing outcomes aren't based on wishful thinking and misguided googling but from proven industry knowledge and solutions you need to know to successfully launch your book into the world. The beauty of this handy resource means you can replicate the process with your second, your third, and all your future books. It's an investment in your writing career for today and tomorrow.

WHAT IS SELF-PUBLISHING?

In this workbook, *self-publishing* is the act of independently publishing your book without waiting months or years to be accepted by a mainstream publishing house. If you want to be an independent author (also known as an *authorpreneur*), then you're actively choosing to pave your own way. You will need to budget for an editor, cover designer, typesetter, and any other industry professional required to improve your book so that it matches industry standards. Authors who choose to self-publish understand that their book is an intellectual property asset, and they commit to a vision of its long-term success and any other personal, creative, or career benefits it has the potential to attract and provide.

The independent approach is also the smartest way to start leveraging yourself in your chosen field or genre. Publishing your own book positions you as an expert and may accelerate career growth, income, and opportunities well beyond what you once believed possible. Authorship translates to authority. When an audience sees you've completed the comprehensive task of writing and launching a book of an exceptional standard, they trust you are dedicated, knowledgeable, and experienced with the subject matter. This is also why it's important to avoid cutting corners on your self-publishing journey. Quality is key and reflects degrees of sophistication and skill, as well as shows that you believe enough in your work to invest in it.

With newly established credibility gained through self-publishing, you may go on to host workshops and programs, charge consulting fees, travel the country or the world speaking publicly, and of course, sell lots of books. You may expand your passion into a high-earning income stream or even a full-time business, creating downloadable products, online courses, and any other resources relative to your expertise, all because you walked the self-publishing path to its completion.

The stigma associated with taking the self-publishing route has lost its grip. Even traditionally published, world-renowned authors such as J. K. Rowling are choosing their independence over mainstream options. Rowling now sells the e-book versions of her Harry Potter series from her website Pottermore.com.

There are too many other success stories to count. After thriller author Mark Dawson's first two traditionally published novels "sank without a trace," and his third novel was rejected by mainstream publishers, he decided to take matters into his own hands and turned to self-publishing. Within just a few years, he has now sold more than four million copies of his 25 books, has made *USA Today* bestseller lists, and enjoys a seven-figure income.

British systems analyst Rachel Abbott was an avid reader of crime fiction, so she decided to try her own hand at it. She wrote *Only the Innocent* on a trip to Italy, and her friends convinced her to self-publish. Within three months of its 2011 release, she'd reached #1 in the entire UK Kindle store after pricing her e-book at 99p during its promotion period. She kept her prices low at £2.99 and attributes her success to the cover line ("Women are rarely cold-blooded killers"), as well as investing in social media marketing. Since then, she has released 11 novels and has sold more than four million copies of her books (McGaw 2021). It really can be that profitable and attainable from the self-publishing springboard.

WHAT YOU WILL LEARN FROM THIS WORKBOOK

The self-publishing journey is about creating *your story, your way*. My clients reflect back to me time and time again that by taking empowered action, they simultaneously awaken a greater sense of purpose and creativity that extends beyond the authorship of their book. It's as though the journey itself evokes discoveries and outcomes that are soul satisfying, enriching, and lead to unexpected and welcome possibilities. My workbook encompasses the fullness of this journey, not just the logistical task of book launching, so when you apply it to your next project, be ready for life-changing results!

Writing a book and publishing it yourself is a personally transformative process and an admirable creative act. It involves unearthing elements of the subconscious, harnessing the power of storytelling, and trusting the mystery of pioneering new ideas as much as it involves collaborating with industry professionals, strategically marketing a new product, and turning your passion into a profitable endeavor. No wonder people get overwhelmed along the way! Thousands of books are self-published every day, yet so many sink to the bottom of the ranks because their quality of production and lack of industry know-how deem the book down-market. Don't let that be you when you can avoid the common mistakes made by hopeful authors regarding how to achieve a successfully self-published book.

Designed in an interactive format, this book is comprised of nine sections that, when followed in order, begin with building creative momentum and end at the arrival of your book launch, its promotion, and celebrating your success as a published author. It steers you on one continuous journey. It will help you discover and refine your book idea and provide advice on planning and structuring it. Tips on writing quickly and efficiently as well as what to look for when hiring the perfect editor are included in its scope. I share with you what to look for when designing a magnetic cover, a seamless layout, and how to plot your marketing strategy for raging success based on doing the hard yards myself in the ever-evolving industries of publishing and marketing. You'll get to focus on your genius—your authorship and the life of your book—with the nuts and bolts of its publication taken care of throughout each section. Saving you hours of trial and error trying to decipher the steps on your own, as well as thousands of dollars investing in misguided advice, *The Self-Publishing Workbook* is both a companion and an esteemed advisor taking a place of pride on the independent author's bookshelf of today.

HOW TO USE THIS WORKBOOK

First, read through the workbook in its entirety to wrap your head around the process. Then return to the beginning and work through it at your own pace. You can complete your goal of writing, publishing, and marketing within a time frame suitable for you. To make the best use of this book:

- ❧ Complete all the prompts, questions, and exercises, and reflect on the inspirational quotes and success stories, especially when you feel stuck or unmotivated. They all play an important part in getting you closer to your goal of becoming a published author.

- ❧ Take it everywhere you go. Have it on hand. Inspiration may strike at any time.

- ❧ Write in it every day. This strengthens your writing habits and maintains the necessary momentum required to actually finish your book. If you use the 10-minute rule and commit to 10 minutes a day, that will quickly amount to hours as you become more engrossed in your creation.

- ❧ Create deadlines for each of your goals and actions and stick to them.

- ❧ Allocate dedicated (uninterrupted!) time to writing your book. If you are working on your book five hours a week, you could be published within six months. The amount of time you can manage is irrelevant. Keep moving forward!

- ❧ Review your workbook regularly to keep yourself on track.

- ❧ Access all the tools and resources recommended throughout this book marked with * at iinspiremedia.com.au/usefulresources.

- ❧ Journal through the creative highs and lows along the way. Writing is a powerful therapeutic tool, and sometimes expressing yourself outside the parameters of your book will create space for more clarity, insight, and solutions. *The Book Inside You*

Journal, the companion to this workbook, may be applied for this very reason—to support you to creatively develop your ideas and clear obstacles on your writing path.

🕉 Celebrate your successes and share your challenges with the online support tribe in *The Heart-Centred Author (Writing, Self-Publishing and Marketing Books)* private Facebook group. Group members can provide valuable feedback for your titles, subtitles, covers, back cover blurbs, and chapter selection, as well as help you with your launch and leave reviews. This need not be a solitary task!

By working diligently through this workbook, you will always be one step closer to celebrating, holding, selling, and cherishing a stunning published book ready to share with the world! All you need to do is commit to and trust in the process.

MY STORY

Today, I am immersed in a dynamic world of self-publishing, authors, workshops, and consulting, yet before you assume I was born with a pen in my hand, let me share my story with you.

It all began in 1998, when I was working in a job in Melbourne, Australia that was draining the life out of me. My real talents were being wasted, and I knew it. I knew there was more to my life, and I had more to offer, even though I didn't yet know what that looked like. So, I quit my job, escaped to London, and reflected on my life to date. What did I *really* want to do? What was my purpose? What was I passionate about?

It became clear to me that I had always loved writing, so I borrowed an old laptop from my neighbor and began writing about things in which I was interested—like people, travel, and food. Every time I wrote a passage of text, I felt alive. The more I practiced writing, the better I honed my craft. I began freelancing for websites and magazines, at first for free and then attracting paid work. In 2001,

I was approached to ghostwrite a book. I didn't even know what ghostwriting was! It involved teaming up with an expert in a certain subject and writing a book for them. I jumped at the chance.

I assisted a personal trainer with his book on health and fitness. This opportunity led to writing a book for a baby signing expert about baby sign language. After that, I helped a spiritual teacher with his book on cosmology, and then wrote a book about dating in your thirties. The projects flowed into my life, yet each time I started writing a book, I experienced feelings of inadequacy and imposter syndrome. Who did I think I was, doing this? I wasn't a writing expert. Then I realized that the more I wrote, the better I became at it. Writing was merely a learned skill that could be developed, refined, and mastered.

In 2005, I returned to Australia and got a job in communications and PR for a deaf children's charity. I discovered that a large number of parents were calling the charity's helpline, desperate for support on raising their deaf and hard-of-hearing children. I discovered that 90% of these children were born to hearing parents with little to no experience with hearing loss. My research showed that, even online, there were no resources available to support these overwhelmed parents, particularly in Australia. So, I took it upon myself to research and write a book on the subject, providing practical tips and strategies for raising a happy, healthy deaf child. I spent the next few months interviewing families, as well as parents of deaf children who were thriving. The result was a book called *Breaking the Sound Barriers: 9 Deaf Success Stories.*

When it came time to publish, however, I ascertained that approximately 1% of manuscripts ever got published. If J. K. Rowling had her first book rejected 14 times by mainstream publishers, *Gone with the Wind* 38 times, *Lord of the Flies* 20 times, and *Chicken Soup for the Soul* 144 times, what hope would a small niche publication like mine have? Even if my book did get picked up by a mainstream publisher, the average time it would take from acceptance to bookshelf would be 18 months. I didn't have years to waste, so I decided to publish the book myself.

I taught myself everything I could about self-publishing. What eventuated was nothing short of amazing. After printing 300 copies on demand, I launched *Breaking the Sound Barriers: 9 Deaf Success Stories* in 2009. The book received over 156 media mentions and was featured on Channel 7 news. It quickly sold out of the first and second print runs. I was hooked! I then pursued online global retailers to sell paperback and e-book versions and traveled to the US and the UK to promote the book. Life became a fabulous adventure, and I was thriving as an independent author.

The sense of joy and accomplishment I gained from self-publishing compelled me to help others on their own journey. In 2010, I began teaching self-publishing at an adult education center in Melbourne, where I taught hundreds of students during a nine-year period. That same year, I created my business, iinspire media, and began mentoring writers to become authors. Since then, my team and I have witnessed hundreds of writers fulfill their publishing dreams and transform their lives along the way. They are now the authors of personal memoirs, cookbooks, self-help workbooks; books about health and wellness, recovering from eating disorders or chronic fatigue; books about hearing loss and cognitive decline; books about business succession planning, project management, immigration, IVF and improving fertility, surviving cancer, and thriving after a divorce. Novels on love and loss, unfulfilled dreams, death, and grief. Children's books about developing a resilient mindset, cultural diversity, environmental, or transgender issues.

Many of my clients have become #1 bestsellers on Amazon in their books' categories, outranking some of the most famous mainstream published authors. Many have had media exposure on TV, radio, and podcasts, or have been interviewed in newspapers, magazines, and blog articles. Some have become global influencers and advocates with large social media followings. Some have built businesses that include booked-out workshops, online programs, consulting, and retreats. Many have gone on to write and self-publish more books once they've experienced the joy of doing it once. And collectively, their books have made a huge impact on tens of thousands of lives, advancing their careers in their respective fields.

I delight in seeing my clients ticking *published author* and *#1 Amazon bestseller* off their bucket lists, proudly holding in their hands a quality book that is making a positive impact around the world, knowing their decision to self-publish assisted them to get where they are today. My bestselling authors, some of whom are generating more than $100K a year in book royalties, are living the lives they once dreamed of. And they all have one thing in common—they started where you are today and made the wise decision backed by informed choices and industry know-how to walk the self-empowered path of author entrepreneurship. *The Self-Publishing Workbook* is my gift to you and a lighthouse for every step of your journey.

So, are you ready?

Strap yourself in and enjoy the ride of your life!

I wish you much joy, inspiration, and success on your journey.

Julie

"If you want to change the world, pick up your pen and write."

—Martin Luther, author of
The Ninety-Five Theses

the prayer I say as I carry the baby away from our home for ever.

It is important to concentrate on anything but the coldness at the heart of the blankets, hardly bigger than the glass paperweight I salvaged from an empty room once.

I place the wrapped-up baby at the bottom of the boat. It isn't hot yet, there is crisp dawn fog where the horizon meets the sea, but I row hard. Normally I would be afraid, but there is no room for that now. My body still aches from last night. I know that disaster can take place despite everything, that there are no guarantees. The sweat drips into my eyes so that the light refracts, and for a second the world explodes around me, and I welcome it. I go as close to the line of buoys as I dare, the water utterly still, and I cradle the baby one last time. There is no answer as I lower my arms into the water up to the elbow. The small parcel falls down through the water.

'I'm giving him back to you,' I tell the sea. Burial at sea. The only honourable option.

Halfway back to shore I judge it safe to stop for a second, and there I draw in the oars and cry harder than I have ever cried before. Harder than after the first razor-shell cut, than the time I fractured my ankle in a fall, than the time I fell asleep in the sun for hours and sunburn burst my skin open and Mother poured salt water over it to stop infection taking hold in my body. I press my hands to my eyes and make a noise that scares me, curl myself up to make the grief more manageable. Our home looms from the shore, and for the first time in a long time, maybe the first time in my life, I do not want to return. But I think about the rest of my family, waiting for me. I think about Llew; maybe he is waiting too. And so I do

1.

START

The German philosopher Fredrich Nietzsche once said, "He who has a *why* to live for can bear almost any *how*." This quote could not be more relevant for writers starting their own journeys. Without knowing the *why* behind what you are doing, you risk losing motivation during the more challenging parts of finishing a book— including getting it over the publishing finish line. Your *why* will boost your motivation and keep you focused along the way. It is the fuel to your creative fire. Your *why* stands tall like a lighthouse, visible in the darkest storm. Knowing your *why* will provide an anchor point to which you can return. If you lose your way or get overwhelmed, your *why* will call you back again and again.

In this chapter, we'll unearth your *why* by asking questions designed to probe deeper beneath the surface and connect you to the intended purpose behind your book. You may discover there are multiple *whys*, or you may end up clarifying a singular focus. Regardless, once you claim it, you'll form a stronger connection with your book that will carry you well into the future. Be open to what the answers may be—they might surprise you!

We'll also be discussing the genre of your book to assist you in starting the writing process with clarity in place from the get-go. The main genres of fiction and nonfiction are categorized into a smorgasbord of subgenres or subcategories, each with specific elements and rules that define them. You'll want to familiarize yourself with these aspects before launching into their territory and may feel inspired to research what's available on the market. It's also important to discover how your actual book idea fits into that genre and subcategory, including its target audience so that it gets discovered and read. I will help you get clear on these elements.

Lastly, when we begin the book-writing journey, you'll want to start with the end in mind—and stay aligned with your dreams. Can you picture your new life as a published author? Now is the time to develop a powerful author vision for your future. So come on, let's dive in! If getting started is the hardest part, then with these markers in place, you'll find you're on a roll as your momentum gathers and creative juices flow. You'll know you're heading in the right direction with solid footing and a clear course from the start.

Why Write a Book?

TO HELP
PEOPLE

TO GET YOUR
MESSAGE
OUT THERE

A NEW ANGLE ON
A SUBJECT

YOU CAN'T FIND A
TOPIC SO YOU WRITE
IT YOURSELF

TO ESTABLISH
YOURSELF IN YOUR
CHOSEN CAREER

TO BECOME
ACKNOWLEDGED AS
THE "EXPERT" IN THAT
SUBJECT

TO GAIN MORE
CLIENTS OR BOOKINGS
FOR A WORKSHOP

TO MAKE
MONEY

Why do you want to write a book?

_____

_____

_____

What are you passionate about in life? What inspires you?

_____

_____

_____

What life experiences have most shaped you?

_____

_____

_____

What are your skills, talents, gifts, abilities, and areas of expertise?

_____

_____

_____

What subjects do you most like to talk about?

_____

_____

_____

What do you love doing that helps others?

_____

_____

_____

What subjects or themes do you most want to write about?

_____

_____

_____

What other subjects or themes could you write about?

_____

_____

_____

Name three books that have made a huge impact on you and why:

_____

_____

_____

What genres of books do you tend to gravitate toward? (See pages 46–48 for a list of genres)

_____

_____

_____

Can you see yourself speaking to the media about your book? Why or why not? What kind of media would you like to do (TV, podcasts, YouTube, etc.)?

_____

_____

_____

Can you see yourself publicly speaking about the subject of your book at book signings, on book tours, or at other events? What would be your main message?

_____

_____

_____

Can you imagine speaking, writing about, and sharing this book on social media, in podcasts, and on blogs? What are some of the messages or themes you'd like to share?

_____

_____

_____

#GENIUS TIP!

Write what you are *passionate* about, not what you think you *should* write.

A student once came into my course wanting to write a book about commercial litigation to leverage his profile. He left my course a far happier version of himself, after writing a Japanese cookbook!

> **Self-Publishing Success Story — Jamie McGuire**
>
> Jamie McGuire received so many rejection letters for her novel *Beautiful Disaster* that, in desperation, she turned to self-publishing it. Within two months, it had sold more than 30,000 copies and had become a *New York Times* bestseller. Atria, an imprint of Simon & Schuster, bought the rights to *Beautiful Disaster*, as well as her next book *Walking Disaster*. Despite her incredible success with a mainstream publisher, she returned to self-publishing and sold her next book *Beautiful Redemption* into Walmart. Since then, she's stayed with self-publishing because in her words, "I am the captain of my own ship" (Coker 2015).

Defining Your Genre

All books are classified as either **FICTION** or **NONFICTION**.

FICTION are books created from your imagination, such as romance, fantasy, thrillers, and science fiction.

NONFICTION are books based in fact, such as business, cookbooks, health and fitness, self-help, true crime, and religion.

Under fiction or nonfiction, you will find many different genres/categories and even subgenres/subcategories within those genres.

Below are the main genres/categories, with their average word counts and an example of each. Circle the ones you most enjoy reading and the one/s you think you'd most enjoy writing.

NONFICTION

SELF-HELP/ PERSONAL GROWTH 30,000–70,000 words Example: *The Road Back to Me: Healing and Recovering from Co-Dependency, Addiction, Enabling, and Low Self-Esteem* by Lisa A. Romano	HEALTH AND FITNESS 30,000–70,000 words Example: *Breath: The New Science of a Lost Art* by James Nestor	CRIME 75,000–120,000 words Example: *Mindhunter: Inside the FBI's Elite Serial Crime Unit* by John E. Douglas and Mark Olshaker
MEMOIR, BIOGRAPHY, AND AUTOBIOGRAPHY 45,000–80,000 words Example: *Becoming* by Michelle Obama	COOKBOOK Word counts vary greatly. Example: *I Quit Sugar: Your Complete 8-Week Detox Program and Cookbook* by Sarah Wilson	HISTORY 30,000–70,000 words Example: *Sapiens: A Brief History of Humankind* by Yuval Noah Harari
TRAVEL 20,000–50,000 words Example: *The Bucket List: 1,000 Adventures Big & Small* by Kath Stathers	HOW TO 3,000–50,000 words Example: *How to Talk to Anyone: 92 Little Tricks for Big Success in Relationships* by Leil Lowndes	ART/ ARCHITECTURE 10,000–60,000 words Example: *The Art of Still Life: A Contemporary Guide to Classical Techniques, Composition, and Painting in Oil* by Todd M. Casey
HUMOR 10,000–50,000 words Example: *Can't Make This Stuff Up: Finding the Upside to Life's Downs* by Susannah B. Lewis	FAMILIES AND RELATIONSHIPS 30,000–50,000 words Example: *What to Expect When You're Expecting* by Heidi Murkoff	CONTEMPORARY 60,000–90,000 words Example: *COVID-19: The Pandemic that Never Should Have Happened and How to Stop the Next One* by Debora MacKenzie

NONFICTION

MOTIVATION/ INSPIRATION	BUSINESS/MONEY ECONOMICS	POLITICS
30,000–70,000 words	30,000–60,000 words	70,000–80,000 words
Example: *Can't Hurt Me: Master Your Mind and Defy the Odds* by David Goggins	Example: *Building a Story Brand: Clarify Your Message So Customers Will Listen* by Donald Miller	Example: *The End of Race Politics: Arguments for a Colorblind America* by Coleman Hughes
TEXTBOOK	CRAFTS, HOME, AND GARDEN	LAW AND CRIMINOLOGY
30,000–70,000 words	30,000–70,000 words	50,000–70,000 words
Example: *Organic Chemistry: Structure and Function* by K. Peter C. Vollhardt and Neil E. Schore	Example: *Spirit of Place: The Making of a New England Garden* by Bill Noble	Example: *The Tools of Argument: How the Best Lawyers Think, Argue, and Win* by Joel P. Trachtman

FICTION

CHILDREN'S BOOKS	ROMANCE	FANTASY
300–1,200 words	55,000–100,000 words	70,000–110,000 words
Example: *Kindness Is My Superpower: A Children's Book About Empathy, Kindness and Compassion* by Alicia Ortego	Example: *For Now, Forever* by Nora Roberts	Example: *A Game of Thrones* by George R. R. Martin
ACTION AND ADVENTURE	HORROR	PARANORMAL
90,000–130,000 words	60,000–90,000 words	60,000–90,000 words
Example: *The Call of the Wild* by Jack London	Example: *Carrie* by Stephen King	Example: *Midnight Sun* by Stephanie Meyer

FICTION

HISTORICAL FICTION	SCIENCE FICTION	SUSPENSE AND THRILLER
60,000–90,000 words	60,000–90,000 words	60,000–110,000 words
Example: *The Help* by Kathryn Stockett	Example: *Hitchhiker's Guide to the Galaxy* by Douglas Adams	Example: *Gone Girl* by Gillian Flynn
MYSTERY	DYSTOPIAN	LITERARY FICTION
40,000–80,000 words	60,000–110,000 words	70,000–100,000 words
Example: *Murder on the Orient Express* by Agatha Christie	Example: *The Hunger Games* by Suzanne Collins	Example: *Anxious People: A Novel* by Fredrik Backman
SHORT STORY COLLECTION	POETRY	NOVELLA
At least 40,000 words, at an average of 2,500 words per story with 16 stories.	30–100 poems	10,000–40,000 words
Example: *The World's Greatest Short Stories* by James Daley (editor)	Example: *The Sun and Her Flowers* by Rupi Kaur	Example: *Close to the Bone* by Kendra Elliot
RELIGION, SPIRITUALITY AND NEW AGE	YOUNG ADULT	COMIC AND GRAPHIC NOVELS
40,000–50,000 words	55,000–90,000 words	20,000–75,000 words
Example: *A Religion of One's Own: A Guide to Creating a Personal Spirituality in a Secular World* by Thomas Moore	Example: *Children of Blood and Bone* by Tomi Adeyemi	Example: *Watchmen* by Alan Moore (Author) and Dave Gibbons (Illustrator)

Subgenres/Subcategories

Each genre/category has subgenres/subcategories. The table below shows the Romance genre and all its subcategories on Amazon. The subcategories under Romance include Historical, Contemporary, Erotic, Regency, Paranormal, Religious/Spiritual, Young Adult, New Adult, and LGBTQ. Then each of these subcategories becomes an even narrower subcategory. For example, Historical Romance niches down further into 20th Century, Ancient World, Medieval, Regency, Renaissance, Tudor, Victorian, or Viking.

GENRE	SUBCATEGORY	SUBCATEGORY
Romance ——————	Action & Adventure	
	Adaptations	
	Alpha Male	
	Amish	
	Billionaires & Millionaires	
	Clean & Wholesome	
	Collections & Anthologies	
	Contemporary	
	Enemies to Lovers	
	Fantasy	
	Gothic	
	Historical ———————————	**Historical**
	Holidays	20th Century
	LGBTQ+	American
	Later in Life	Ancient World
	Literature & Fiction	Gilded Age
	Love Triangle	Medieval
	Mafia Romance	Regency
	Multicultural & Interracial	Renaissance
	New Adult & College	Scottish
	Paranormal	Tudor
	Polyamory	Victorian
	Rockstar Romance	Viking
	Romance in Uniform	
	Romantic Comedy	
	Romantic Suspense	
	Science Fiction	
	Small Town Romance	
	Sports	
	Time Travel	
	Western & Frontier	
	Workplace Romance	

Figure 1.
Table showing the Romance genre and subcategories on Amazon.com

Write down two genres/categories in which you'd like to write. Then write down some possible subgenres/subcategories you'd consider writing in. The narrower your niche, the more likely you are to be discovered and read.

Example:

GENRE	SUBCATEGORY
Romance	*Historical romance (Regency era)*
	Paranormal vampire romance
	Religious romance

GENRE	SUBCATEGORY

It is important to know the genre/category and subgenre/subcategory in which you'll be writing to ensure your ideal readers find your book and read it. Each has its own set of specific elements, rules, and expectations. Not knowing these may result in disappointed readers and poor reviews. So, get to know your genre and subcategories by reading books in them and understanding their elements, rules, and covers. Find out what readers love (and don't) by reading testimonials from bestselling books in those subcategories. You can learn a lot.

**Remember, you don't have to be a brilliant
writer to be a bestseller!**

Everything Men Know About Women by Dr. Alan Francis and Cindy Cashman is blank and has sold over 1 million copies!

35,000 Baby Names is just a list of baby names and has sold 100,000 copies.

All I Need to Know I Learned from My Cat by Suzy Becker has sold 1.6 million copies.

What ideas come to you now?

_____

_____

_____

_____

**Who would have ever thought that these books would
dominate the bestselling charts on Amazon for several years?**

The adult coloring book *Secret Garden* by Johanna Basford has sold more than 12 million copies.

The Life-Changing Magic of Tidying Up by Marie Kondo has sold more than 9 million copies.

The *4 Ingredients Cookbook,* a black-and-white book with no pictures by Rachel Birmingham and Kim McCosker, has sold more than 9 million copies.

When you have answered these questions, you should have a good idea about the sort of book you'd like to write.

What is your book idea?

_____

_____

_____

_____

_____

_____

_____

_____

Self-Publishing Success Story —Lisa Genova

Lisa Genova wrote the novel *Still Alice* when her grandmother started struggling with Alzheimer's. Lisa could no longer stand the rejection letters from literary agents and took matters into her own hands, self-publishing her book in 2007. She then spent the next two years selling print-on-demand copies of her book and discussion guides to promote conversations about Alzheimer's. In 2009, the book was picked up by Simon & Schuster and sold 2.6 million copies in 30 languages. It went onto to be adapted into an Oscar-winning film starring Julianne Moore and Alec Baldwin (Genova 2015).

"Writing is the only thing that, when I do it, I don't feel I should be doing something else."

—Gloria Steinem, author of *My Life on the Road* and *Revolution from Within*

Developing Your Book Idea

Jot down three to six possible ideas for books based on your answers on previous pages. Come up with actual book ideas. For example,

"I want to write a historical crime thriller set in the years after World War II where a detective is trying to catch an escaped Nazi."

Or

"My idea for a book is a cookbook that blends together South African cuisine with soul food from the Southern states of the US."

1. _____

_____

2. _____

_____

3. _____

_____

Choose the idea that most appeals to you. I understand you may never have written a 50,000-word novel before, but if you love reading crime thrillers and you're excited to write one, just know it can be done!

_____

_____

_____

_____

_____

_____

Who is your ideal reader or readers? Be as specific as possible. This group/s will become your *target audience*. See the table below.

_____

_____

_____

_____

WHAT DOES *TARGET AUDIENCE* MEAN?

The *target audience* or *target readers* or *target market* are the group of people who would be the most helped or entertained by your book.

For example, the target market for a book about getting newborns to sleep would be new moms aged 20–40 who are desperate to get their babies to sleep. The readers for a young adult novel would be teenagers aged 12–18. And the readers of romance novels are mostly women in their 40s.

Have you seen any books similar to the one you'd like to write? E.g., If you want to write about a book about surviving anorexia, what other books have you found out there on this topic?

_____

_____

_____

_____

_____

_____

What did you like about these similar books? (e.g., the attractive covers, the way they dealt with the topic, the illustrations, the case studies). What was missing (e.g., they failed to include x and y topics and their personal story was weak)?

_____

_____

_____

_____

_____

_____

Self-Publishing Success Story —Sergio de la Pava

Manhattan public defense lawyer Sergio de la Pava wrote a raging 688-page critique of the total lack of justice in the criminal justice system in 2008. For two years he searched for an agent, but no one was willing to take on a book of that length, so he gave up. His wife, Susanna, on the other hand, did not. She self-published 100 copies and sent them out for reviews. In October 2010, _The Quarterly Conversation_ called it "one of the best and most original novels of the decade." The University of Chicago Press published the book as a paperback in 2012, and it was named one of the 10 best works of fiction in 2012 (Sandler 2013).

Create Your Powerful Author Vision

Once you are clear on your *why*, it's important to envision your life as a published author. Imagine a day two years from now when you have accomplished your dream and are now a successful author. What would that look like for you? Be as specific as possible. Where would you be? What are you doing? What are you creating? Who is with you? How and where are you spending your time? How are you feeling about yourself? Having a unique, compelling vision pulls you toward your destination and is critical in getting you there.

Example: It is June 18 [write a year two years from now]. I am loving my new life as a published author. My book launch was one of the proudest and happiest days of my life. I could make out the smiling faces of my family, friends, and colleagues during my speech as they cheered and clapped for me in the large crowd. Signing copies of my book for those who lined up to congratulate me was an experience I will never forget. Since the launch, the book has taken off. It hit #1 in Amazon in several categories, and I've already sold 5,000 books. The book has been featured on morning television programs and in several metropolitan newspapers. I've been interviewed on a few prestigious TV shows and podcasts. I've been doing book signings and talks at various shops, libraries, and events. Whenever I share my book on social media, I get lots of likes, congratulatory comments, and sales. I've been able to leave my full-time job and am now engaged in well-paid part-time consulting work, which allows me to spend more time on writing more books and more time with my family. I've started creating online courses, one-day workshops, and a Bali retreat. I've been traveling the country speaking and inspiring people about mindfulness. This has been a dream come true!

My powerful author vision is:

_____

_____

_____

_____

_____

_____

_____

_____

_____

_____

How are you going to feel when you have your published book in your hands?

- [ ] Elated

- [ ] Joyful

- [ ] Blissful

- [ ] Sense of achievement

Holding a copy of your printed book in your hands will be one of the most memorable moments of your life. How are you going to celebrate when you are holding your book in your hands? Will you take time to reflect on all the hard work it took to get there? Will you share the joy with friends, family, and supporters? Will you reward yourself with a treat of a massage, or a weekend away with your loved one/s? How will you be feeling? The more specific you are, the more likely it will happen.

_____

_____

_____

_____

_____

_____

"A goal without a plan is just a wish."

—Antoine de Saint-Exupéry,
author of *The Little Prince*

2.

PLAN

"Vision without action is merely a dream. Action without vision just passes the time. Vision with action can change the world."

—Joel A. Barker, author of *Paradigms*

Have You Got a Plan?

When it comes to creating a book comprised of a variety of elements, you will set yourself up for success by plotting out the details as thoroughly as you can from the beginning. This will support your dream becoming a reality.

There's no need to reinvent the wheel when it comes to planning your book. In this chapter, I will prompt you with questions about important aspects that need to be considered when producing a published book. Knowing these elements will give shape to the final product in its entirety, from the cover design to the blurb to any research you may need to conduct. My questions are designed to get you thinking—or *percolating*, as I like to call it—over the finer details of your creation. The devil really is in the details, and if you work through each aspect early, you'll find you are much more organized rather than scrambling to finalize the essential components toward the end. Give yourself the gift of time to thoughtfully contemplate these areas. Your care will be reflected in the overall quality of your finished book.

I encourage you to work through this chapter by casting your attention on each area one at a time. Together, we'll unpack your title and subtitle, target audience, your author name or pseudonym, visualizing and finalizing the book cover and interior design, writing the back cover blurb, chapter structure, resources and references, and clarifying your author bio. The wonderful part of self-publishing means you have control over all these elements—*you* decide! So, enjoy this opportunity to really go for what you want to create in terms of how you and your book are represented in the world. Some people get bogged down in the details or find it difficult to persevere with the process. If you can stick with it and see this as a rewarding process, then I believe you will enjoy taking ownership of these necessary finishing touches to your beautiful book.

WHAT IS THE WORKING TITLE OF YOUR BOOK?

Your working title doesn't have to be your final title. It merely gives you a good starting point for your book. It needs to be short, catchy, and memorable—ideally two to three words—and tell your readers *exactly* what the book is about, and/or what outcome they will get by reading your book, e.g., *Public Relations Disasters*, *Master Your Emotions*, or *Declutter Your Mind*. Ideally, your title should contain the keywords a potential reader will be typing into the Amazon search bar or other search engines to find a book like yours. Creating a cryptic title that is clever to you but is confusing to your audience will hinder rather than help your sales. Please read *The Amazon Algorithm* below before you create your title, as this will help you enormously in giving your book more visibility and sales.

My book's working title is:

_____

_____

WHAT IS THE SUBTITLE?

If you have a nonfiction book, then your book needs a subtitle. Your subtitle should tell the reader *exactly* what the book is about and eliminate any confusion, e.g., *How to Protect Yourself from Workplace Psychopaths*. If you haven't included your main keywords in the title, you should most definitely put them in the subtitle. And if you have already included your main keyword in the title, then include more keywords in your subtitle.

If you are writing fiction, you may type *A Page-Turning Suspense Thriller with a Terrifying Climax* or *A Gripping WWII Novel with an Emotional Twist* into the subtitle metadata when you publish on the publishing platforms. This not only gives your audience a clear idea of what your book is about but makes your book easier to find when people are searching for books like yours. See *The Amazon Algorithm* below.

My book's subtitle is:

_____

_____

_____

THE AMAZON ALGORITHM

Seventy percent of global book sales come from Amazon. Amazon works like Google in that it is a giant search engine. When customers are looking for a book, they may type keywords or phrases such as *children's books about resilience* into the search engine. If your title, subtitle, and book description contain the keywords people regularly type into the Amazon search engine to find books like yours, your book is far more likely to rank at the top of the Amazon listings. If your title, subtitle, and book description don't contain relevant keywords, then your book is likely to stay buried among the millions of other books on Amazon.

Rather than trying to be clever or mysterious with your title and subtitle or use puns or metaphors, think about what customers will be searching for when they are looking for a book like yours and then incorporate these words into your title and subtitle.

For example: *My Strong Mind: A Children's Book About Developing Mental Strength* (for a children's book), or *Opshopulence: How to Make Thrift Store Look like Couture and Save the Planet* (nonfiction book), or for a novel, *The Newlyweds: A Completely Gripping Psychological Thriller with a Jaw-Dropping Twist.*

In order to easily find the most searched keywords for your niche, I recommend using Publisher Rocket*. Here is a link: https://iinspiremedia--rocket.thrivecart.com/publisher-rocket/

Publisher Rocket* is the best software on the market today. It will not only help you find hundreds of profitable keywords in your niche in a few seconds, but it will also show your competitors' books, what they are earning per month, and the best categories in your genre. Using this tool will save you valuable time and money in putting out a book that won't get seen and won't sell. I use it for all my clients' books, and at a single payment of US$199 (as of this publication date), it's worth every cent.

Look for the keywords that have a high search volume (ideally more than 1,000 Amazon searches per month) with "medium" or "low" competition (ideally a competitive score of less than 80) on Publisher Rocket*. Keywords are two-to-four-word phrases such as *resilience children's books* or *income generating tips*. Try to put these keywords into your title, subtitle, and book description. Ideally, the main keyword/s will go at the beginning of your title. Next best is in the subtitle, and then the book description. Sprinkle your keywords as naturally as possible throughout your book description.

Please read Amazon's guidelines on titles and subtitles to ensure you don't break any of their rules.

Your keywords can also go into the Keywords section on the publishing platforms we use. (See *Publishing* for more on this). This is what's known as "optimizing" your listing on Amazon, and optimization is how you can rank in the Top 10 on Amazon in one of your subcategories!

WHO IS YOUR BOOK'S IDEAL TARGET AUDIENCE?

Hint: If you try and write your book for everyone, you write for no one. Visualize your ideal reader right down to their age, gender, interests, and location. What problem/s are they facing right now? For example, your target reader may be someone who is female, aged 30–35, married, a stay-at-home mom to her first child, loves parenting books, and is desperate to solve her toddler's meltdowns. When you write for everyone, you appeal to no one. The more you speak directly to your ideal reader, the better your book will be.

My book's target audience is:

_____

_____

_____

_____

_____

USING A PSEUDONYM OR "PEN NAME" AS YOUR AUTHOR NAME

Using a pen name or a pseudonym rather than your real name as your author name is a personal choice. To help you decide the right path for you, here are some pros and cons to using a pseudonym:

PROS

1. You can write whatever you want without other people—your family, your boss, your coworkers—knowing it's you. For example, you can write erotic fiction or about your painful divorce without having to worry about your boss or ex-spouse finding out.

2. You may have a name that is long and difficult to spell or pronounce.

3. You share the same name as another famous author.

4. You are writing in two or three different genres such as nonfiction and fiction, or nonfiction and children's books, and you want to make a clear distinct name for yourself in each genre.

CONS

Hiding your identity makes it more difficult (but not impossible) to market your book, particularly with nonfiction. If you're writing a nonfiction book as the expert, people need to see the expert and your level of expertise in the field. To effectively get your book out there, you're going to have to speak about your book on TV, radio, podcasts, social media, YouTube, etc. If you are going to use an alias with your nonfiction book, you can however still market your book using Amazon and Facebook ads. It's also much easier to write and market fiction than nonfiction under a pseudonym. You can set up social media handles under your pseudonym and then market your fiction book with Facebook, Instagram, and Amazon ads.

Will you be using your own name as the author name, or will you use a pseudonym? What will your author name/pseudonym be?

_____

_____

_____

_____

_____

_____

YOUR BACK COVER

Writing the back cover before you've written the book will help you with your end vision. What will your back cover say? Have a look at books in your genre and subgenre for ideas. Read lots of back cover blurbs in your genre. Search for the bestselling titles, as they are obviously doing something right.

EXAMPLE OF A NONFICTION BACK COVER BLURB

Figure 2. Front and back cover of *The Self-Publishing Workbook*, showing breakdown of elements.

TIPS FOR YOUR NONFICTION BACK COVER

1. Write a captivating headline at the top. This could be a statement such as: *An invaluable resource for sufferers of anorexia.* Or it could be a question such as: *Despite constant efforts to declutter, does your home still resemble a tangled mess of noodles?* Or a testimonial such as: *The most invaluable resource for sufferers of eating disorders.* —Richard Thao, CEO of Eating Disorder Organization.

2. Create a compelling 250-word description that includes five benefits your readers will gain from reading your book. It's a good idea to sprinkle your main keywords (the words that customers type into Amazon to find a book like yours) naturally throughout this book description, as this book description will later go on your Amazon page and will help you to show up in the Amazon search results listings.

3. Always write in the third person ("he", "she" or "they"), not in the first person ("I" or "me"), as if a copywriter had written it, not you.

4. The back cover should also contain a short, catchy author bio of no more than four sentences.

5. Add one or two of your best testimonials for social proof.

6. It is preferable (but not essential) to include a professional photo next to your bio so your audience can see the person who has written the book.

7. Have a look at the one on the previous page.

EXAMPLE OF A FICTION BACK COVER BLURB

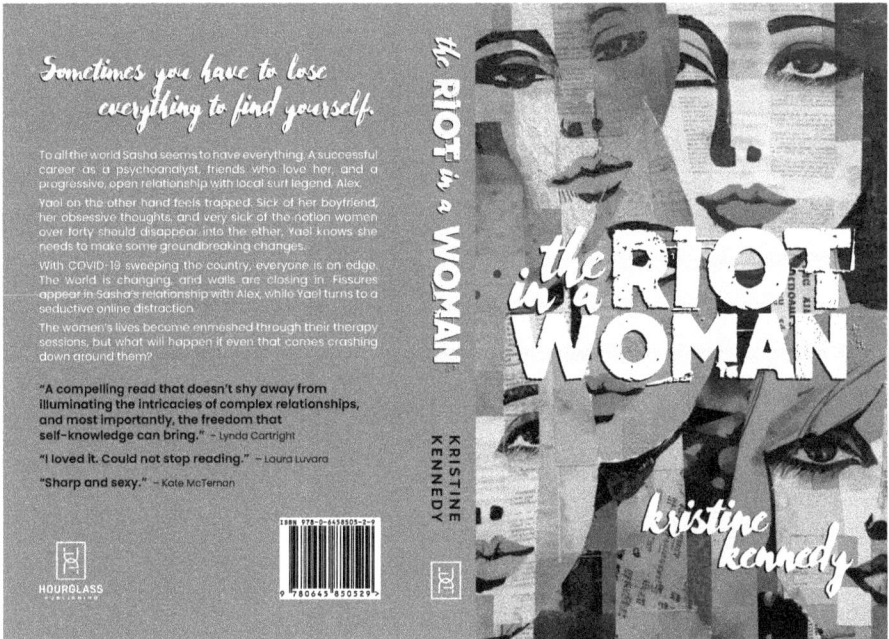

Figure 3. Front and back cover of *The Riot in a Woman* by Kristine Kennedy, copyright 2023. Reproduced with kind permission from Kristine Kennedy and Hourglass Publishing.

TIPS FOR YOUR FICTION BACK COVER

1. Write a compelling headline to draw in your readers. This needs to be a statement such as the one above: *Sometimes you have to lose everything to find yourself.*

2. Write it in the third person, not the first person, e.g., *Sasha seems to have everything*. Remember to write it as if you are the marketing person, not the author.

3. Keep the blurb no more than 250 words.

4. Write in present tense.

5. Use powerful, emotive words such as *tormented, passion, obsession,* and *terrifying.*

6. Don't give away subplots. Keep your readers wanting to read your book!

7. Most fiction books do not have an author bio on the back cover, although you'll need a short author bio for your Amazon, Goodreads, and other online profiles later. Have a look at bestselling books in your genre and emulate what they do.

8. Put one or two testimonials on the back.

EXAMPLE OF A CHILDREN'S BOOK BACK COVER BLURB

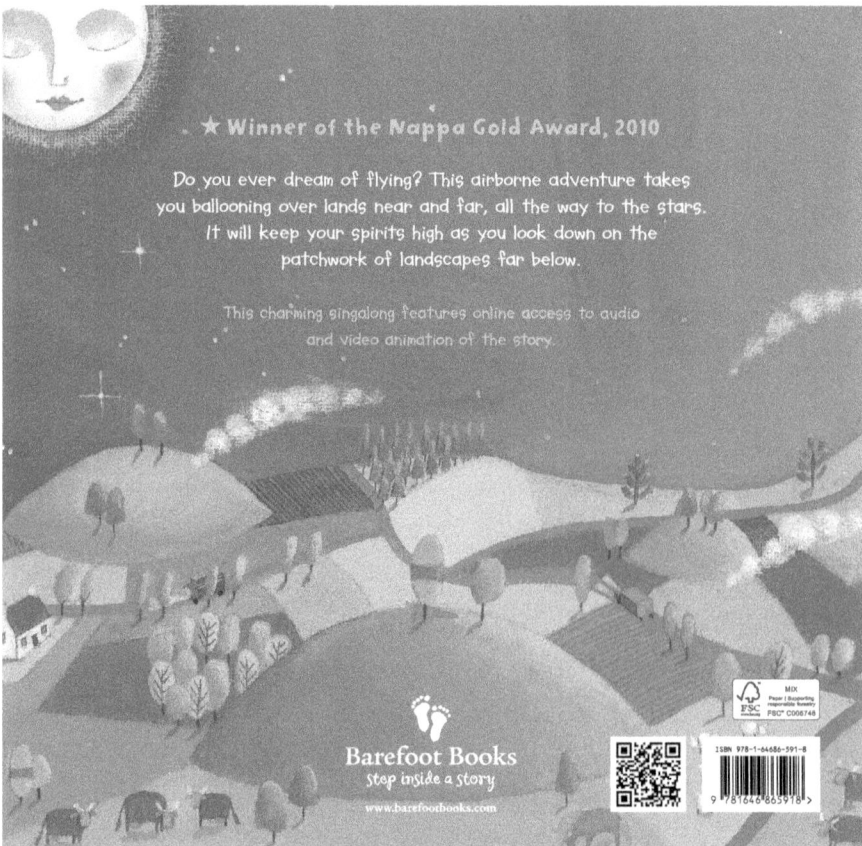

Figure 4. Back cover of *Up, Up, Up!* by Susan Reed and illustrated by Rachel Oldfield, copyright 2022. Reproduced with kind permission from Susan Reed, Rachel Oldfield, and Barefoot Books

TIPS FOR YOUR CHILDREN'S BOOK BACK COVER

1. Have a short but compelling blurb at the back of the book. Have a look at the back covers of some children's books for examples and inspiration, such as the one on page 72.

2. Speak directly to engage the parent and the child.

3. Your back cover blurb is far shorter than the book description you will write for Amazon and other book retailers. Your Amazon book description will be around 600 words compromising of a compelling headline, selling the benefits of the book to the parents, a summary of the story, and 2-3 testimonials.

Your Back Cover Blurb

It's time to write yours!

YOUR COMPELLING HEADLINE

Example from the back cover of my book, *Breaking the Sound Barriers: 9 Deaf Success Stories*:

An invaluable resource for parents of deaf and hard-of-hearing children.

Now it's your turn! What is *your* compelling headline?

_____

_____

_____

Your Enticing Book Description

Example from the back cover of *Emotional Intelligence: Why It Can Matter More than IQ* by Daniel Goleman:

Everyone knows that high IQ is no guarantee of success, happiness, or virtue, but until Emotional Intelligence, *we could only guess why. Daniel Goleman's brilliant report from the frontiers of psychology and neuroscience offers startling new insight into our "two minds"—the rational and the emotional—and how they together shape our destiny.*

Through vivid examples, Goleman delineates the five crucial skills of emotional intelligence and shows how they determine our success in relationships, work, and even our physical well-being. What emerges is an entirely new way to talk about being smart.

The best news is that "emotional literacy" is not fixed early in life. Every parent, every teacher, every business leader, and everyone interested in a more civil society has a stake in this compelling vision of human possibility.

What is your enticing book description?

_____

_____

_____

_____

_____

_____

_____

_____

Your Short Author Bio

A short author bio is needed for the back cover of a nonfiction book and commonly goes on the back page of the inside of a fiction book. A children's book usually doesn't contain an author bio, but you'll need to write one for the Amazon page.

You'll need to write a longer About the Author bio that goes on one of the front pages or one of the back pages of your nonfiction book, but let's focus on that later.

Example:

This short author bio can be found on the back cover of *Chill and Prosper: The New Way to Grow Your Business, Make Millions, and Change the World* by Denise Duffield-Thomas (Duffield-Thomas 2022).

Denise Duffield-Thomas is an award-winning speaker, author and entrepreneur, a lazy self-made millionaire, and an unbusy mother of three children. As a money mindset mentor, she helps women release their fear of money, set premium prices for their services, and take back control over their finances. Find her at www.deniseDT.com, Instagram: @denisedt.

In your short author bio, include anything that builds your authority on your book's subject or builds your credibility in general. Mention any books you have previously written. If you don't have any relevant qualifications or experience and no previously published books, don't stress! Mention anything quirky or authentic to which readers can relate.

Author, R. W. Ridley wrote the following as part of his bio in his first book, *The Takers: Book One of the Oz Chronicles*, and was surprised to find that people would read the back, laugh, and buy the book:

R. W. Ridley lives in Charleston, South Carolina with his beautiful wife, a hyperactive dog, three arrogant cats, and one ugly mortgage.

Now it's your turn!

My short author bio for the back cover of my nonfiction book is:

_____

_____

_____

_____

Questions for Your Fiction Book

What is your genre/category and subgenre/subcategory?

_____

_____

What are the expectations of that genre/category (word count, images, etc.)?

_____

_____

_____

What is your story? (On a separate document, write a one-page outline of your story with beginning, climax, and resolution.)

_____

_____

_____

_____

Who are your characters? On a separate document, write a summary of each character.

_____

_____

_____

_____

_____

What are your story's settings? On a separate document, write details of each setting.

_____

_____

_____

_____

_____

_____

What are your themes?

_____

_____

_____

_____

_____

_____

_____

Questions for Your Children's Book

Which age group are you writing for: 0–3 year olds, 2–5 year olds, 3–7 year olds, 4–8 year olds, 5–10 year olds, or 7–12 year olds? The books in each age group will have a different word count. Have a look at the table below.

WORD COUNTS OF CHILDREN'S BOOKS

0–200 words	Ages 0–3	Board Book
200–500 words	Ages 2–5	Early Picture Book
500–800 words	Ages 3–7	Picture Book
600–1,000 words	Ages 4–8	Older Picture Book
3,000–10,000 words	Ages 5–10	Chapter Book
10,000–30,000 words	Ages 7–12	Middle Grade

Choose one age group and its appropriate word count, then write a book that contains age-appropriate vocabulary for them.

Who are your characters and what is your storyline? Choose characters and a storyline to which your child reader can relate.

_____

_____

_____

_____

_____

_____

Remember that parents are the buyers of children's books and tend to buy books that teach something valuable to their child. What story can you create that is enjoyable and engaging for the child *and* that contains a powerful lesson?

_____

_____

_____

_____

_____

_____

_____

_____

The most common children's book category is Picture Books for 3–7 Year Olds. This is usually a book of around 32 pages that relies on both words and illustrations to tell the story. Aim for 500–800 words. We will look for an illustrator later (see page 177) but think about how the book can be illustrated as single- and double-page spreads.

_____

_____

_____

_____

_____

_____

_____

Questions for Your Nonfiction Book

How many chapters will your nonfiction book have? Using a mind map, create the outline of your book like the one below.

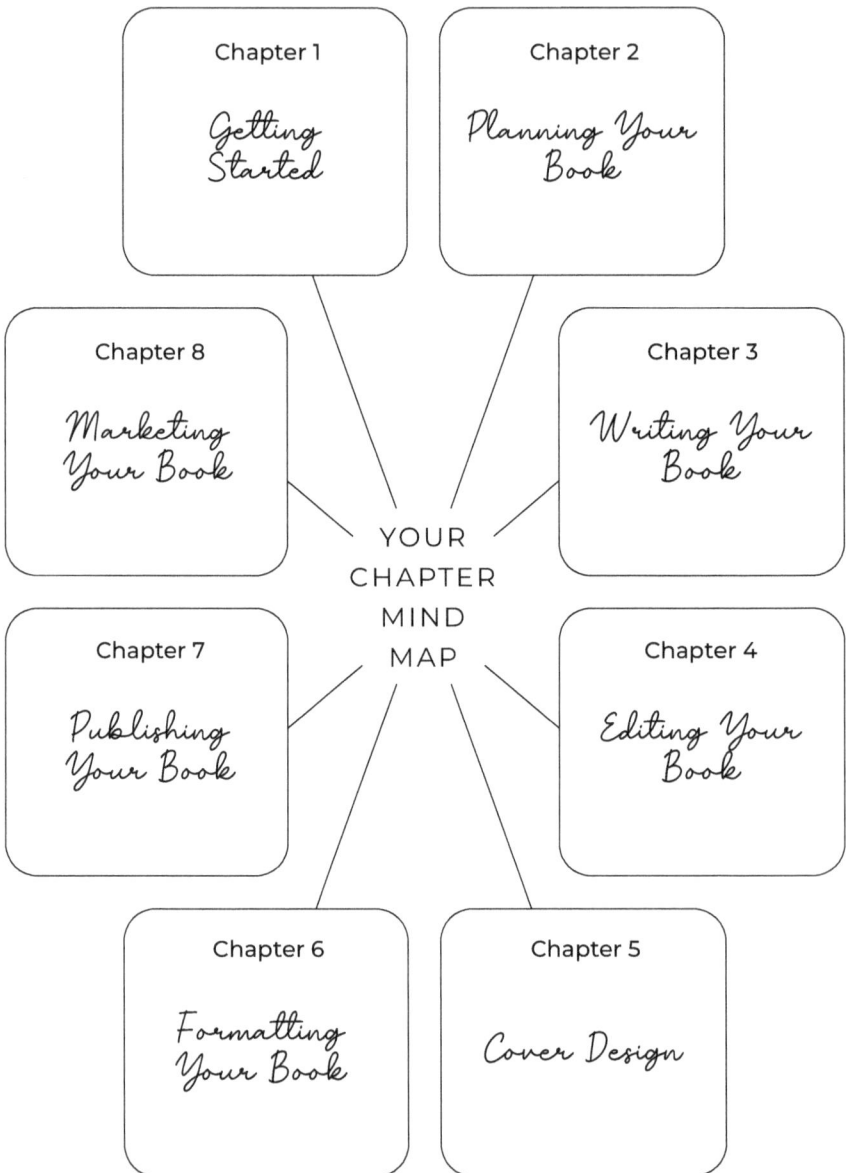

Chapter 1
Getting Started

Chapter 2
Planning Your Book

Chapter 8
Marketing Your Book

Chapter 3
Writing Your Book

YOUR
CHAPTER
MIND
MAP

Chapter 7
Publishing Your Book

Chapter 4
Editing Your Book

Chapter 6
Formatting Your Book

Chapter 5
Cover Design

YOUR
CHAPTER
MIND
MAP

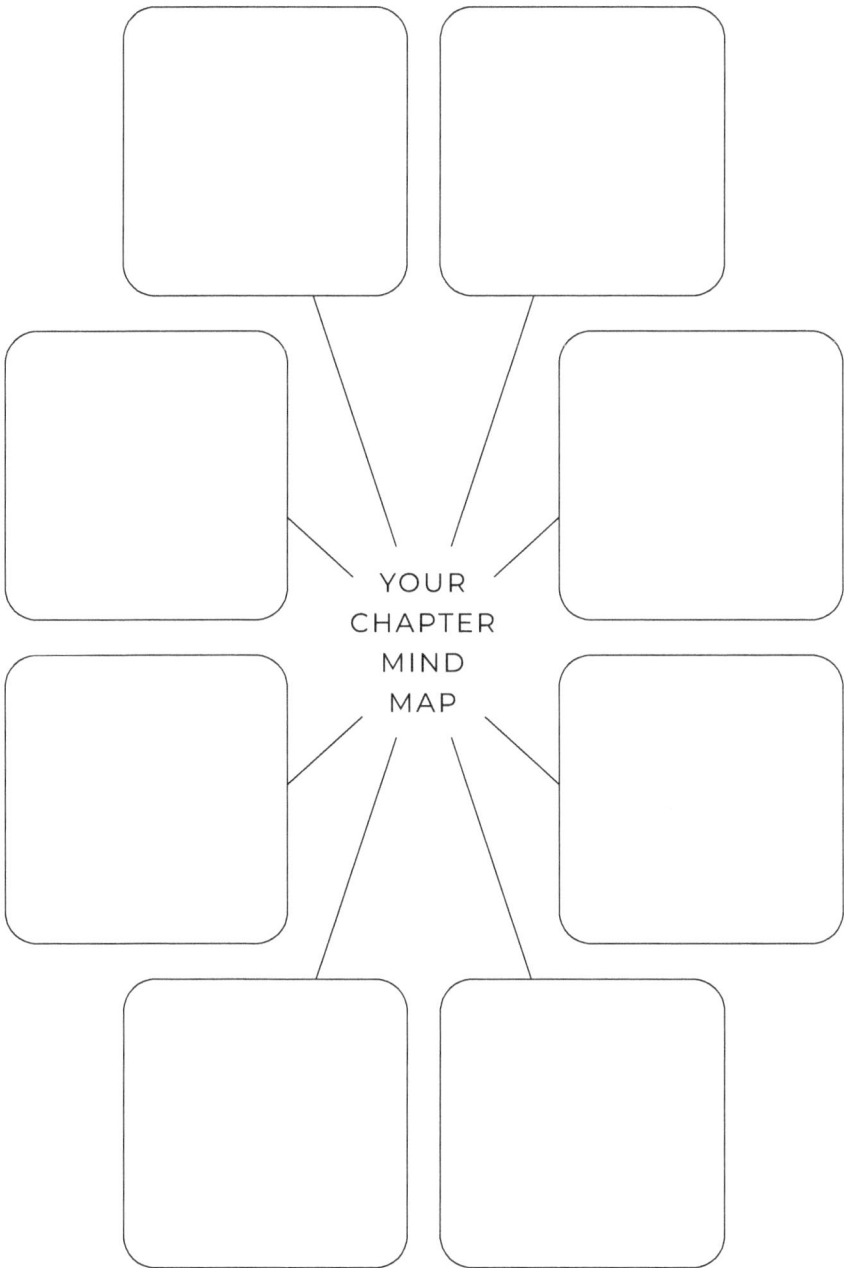

Underneath each of your chapter headings above, write down 10 topics you'll cover in each chapter.

Is your book going to have case studies?

_____

What's the tone going to be? Lighthearted? Academic? Conversational?

_____

Is it going to include quotes from famous people, books or other publications, or song lyrics?

_____

Do you envision lots of headings and bullet points?

_____

Will you need to do interviews?

_____

Do You Need to Seek Permission to Use Material?

Writers frequently refer to, extract, and quote from other sources in the course of their writing.

1. THE UNITED STATES

Paraphrasing/Summarizing/Referencing

In the US, materials that are paraphrased, summarized, or referenced without being *quoted* can simply include a citation and do not require permission to "reprint" or "reproduce," because you are not including the specific wording of another writer (or art from another creator). However, quoting or excerpting passages from published materials may require you to request permission to reprint so you do not violate any copyright laws.

Public Domain

It is best to start with the assumption that anything published in the past 70 years is protected by copyright law. Be prepared to request permission to reprint any copyright-protected quotes, excerpts, or visuals you want to include in your book. If a publication is older than 70 years, it is in the "public domain," and you will not have to seek permission to reprint anything from it. Public domain works also include materials published by the US government, such as photos published by NASA, for example, which do not require permission to reprint.

Fair Use

Some uses of copyright-protected material are included under "fair use laws," and if the material you want to include is considered fair use, you will not need permission to reprint it, but be wary: one of the determining factors for whether reprinted material is "fair use" is whether it's being used for *commercial purposes*. Since you likely want to use quotes, excerpts, or images in a book you're planning to *sell*, a judge could ultimately consider your use of someone else's material as copyright infringement, which comes with hefty fines beginning at US$30,000 per violation. Under fair use laws, small portions of copyrighted material can be used for the purposes of *education, criticism, commentary, news reporting,* and *scholarly reporting.* You may be able to argue that your use of a quote is "educational," for example, if the copyright holder seeks legal action against you.

Epigraphs—short quotes at the beginning of book chapters or sections—may be considered "fair use" if they are directly connected and referred to in the text that follows them. For more information, take a look at pages 9–10 of *Copyright, Fair Use, and Obtaining Permissions for Your Book Guidelines for Authors* from Duke University Press.

Requesting Permission

To secure permission to reprint a quote, excerpt, or visual image, first determine who holds the copyright to the material. For most books, the copyright holder is the publisher, whose information can be found on the copyright page. If it's not immediately clear who holds the copyright, the US Copyright Office at Copyright.gov can help. You may want to download their publication *How to Investigate the Copyright Status of a Work*.

Once you have determined the copyright holder, contact them in writing to obtain permission to use their words or images in your book. Your request should include as many details as possible, such as the specific quote/excerpt for which you're requesting permission, how it will be used, and in what context. The University of Chicago Press provides an excellent, free template request letter on their website.

The copyright holder has the right to decline or limit your use of their materials, or they may charge you to reprint their materials. So, be prepared for a variety of responses. You should also have a backup plan in case the copyright holder never responds. It's common for publishers to take *four to eight weeks* to respond to reprint requests, but there is no legal requirement for them to respond at all. If you don't get a response, your request is denied, or the copyright holder wants to charge more than you want to pay, you may want to consider using a different quote or simply summarizing the material and citing it as a reference rather than quoting from it directly.

2. CANADA

Similar to US copyright laws, Canadian copyright laws do not require authors to seek permission to include summaries, paraphrases, or references to copyrighted materials; just include the appropriate citations. The Canadian public domain and "fair dealing" (i.e., "fair use") laws are similar to the US, with "fair dealing" exceptions allowing you to use other people's materials for the purposes of *research, private study, criticism, review or news reporting, education,* and *satire or parody.*

Should you need to seek permission to reprint materials, Canadian copyright law grants copyright first and foremost to the author/creator of the material, and secondly, to the publisher of that material. Contact the copyright holder with a detailed request, and be prepared for a delay of up to several months to receive a response. Similar to US copyright laws, if you do not obtain a license to reuse the material, you should not reprint that material and should be prepared with an alternative.

For more information, visit the Canadian Copyright Office website, the "Copyright Basics" page on the website for Toronto Metropolitan University, and the page on "Canadian Copyright Law" from the University of Alberta.

3. THE UK

In the UK, copyrighted works enter the public domain 70 years after the author's death and are protected by copyright during that time. UK copyright laws allow writers the same kind of fair dealing of other's materials as Canada, as long as the original works are acknowledged and only a small number of words are quoted. If your use of another creator's material does not fall under a "fair dealing" exception and you must contact the copyright holder for permission to reuse their material, it is common practice for UK copyright holders to charge a royalty percentage based on your sales.

For more information, see "Obtaining Permission to Use Copyright Material" on the UK Copyright Service website as well as the publication "Exceptions to Copyright: Guidance for Consumers" from the UK Intellectual Property Office Online.

4. AUSTRALIA

Under the terms of the Australian Copyright Act 1968, a writer needs to seek permission from the original copyright holder to use any material he or she has quoted, regardless of the length or purpose for the quote or extract, unless the work is not in copyright (70 years after the death of the creator or the date of first publication, whatever comes last). Advice: Make all reasonable attempts to contact the copyright holder and keep correspondence on file. Even if you don't receive a response, someone can see you've made efforts to do so. In all cases, please acknowledge your sources both in the body of the text, as above, and in your References at the back of your book.

For example, you can acknowledge your source in the body of the text by writing this:

In his book, *Wisdom of the Ages*, author Wayne Dyer writes, "When you see yourself connected to everyone, you immediately cease your judgment of the other..."

Then place it in your References at the back of the book like this:

Dyer, Wayne W. 1999. *Wisdom of the Ages: Eternal Truths for Everyday Life*. London: Thorsons, 71.

Do you have permission to use case studies and quotes?

_____

_____

_____

_____

#GENIUS TIP—PLAN A *SERIES!*

Many successful authors have a series of books rather than just a standalone book. Some write books in different genres under different author names.

If you are writing a nonfiction book, consider splitting your 50,000-word book into a series of smaller books of between 10,000–20,000 words. Not only will these be quicker for you to write and publish, but they will also be easier to digest for your reader. This will expand your audience and improve your sales.

If you are writing fiction, how could you break up the storyline and create a series?

If you are writing a children's book, could you do a series around the same theme or character?

If your readers like one of your books in the series, then they will buy the rest, giving you a better income. Not only this, but Amazon will also market the others in your series to them, which is free marketing for you.

Does your book lend itself to a series?

_____

_____

_____

_____

_____

_____

Self-Publishing Success Story—Andy Weir

Computer programmer Andy Weir tried to get publishers and agents interested in his book to no avail. So, he started posting his book *The Martian* on his personal blog one chapter at a time. Then he decided to put it all together and publish it as an e-book for US99¢ on Amazon. That's when things took off. First, it became #1 in the science fiction category. Then, he reached the *New York Times* Bestseller list in hardcover fiction. After that, he signed a six-figure deal with Crown Publishing and Twentieth Century Fox as his book was turned into a feature film starring Matt Damon (Wisconsin Public Radio 2015).

"It is not the critic who counts; not the man who points out how the strong man stumbles, or where the doer of deeds could have done them better. The credit belongs to the man who is actually in the arena, whose face is marred by dust and sweat and blood; who strives valiantly; who errs, who comes short again and again, because there is no effort without error and shortcoming; but who does actually strive to do the deeds; who knows great enthusiasms, the great devotions; who spends himself in a worthy cause; who at the best knows in the end the triumph of high achievement, and who at the worst, if he fails, at least fails while daring greatly, so that his place shall never be with those cold and timid souls who neither know victory nor defeat."

—Theodore Roosevelt, president of the US and author of 35 books including *The Rough Riders* and *The Strenuous Life*

THE LIFE YOU'VE
AYS DREAMED OF.
FEARLESS IN THE
E OF ADVERSITY.
R STOP LEARNING.
YOUR IMAGINATION
NEVER POSSIBLE.
GNIZE THE   AUTY
SURROUN
EMBER WHI
E FROM, BU
E SIGHT OF
YOU ARE GO

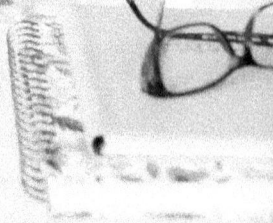

3.

WRITE

"Write it. Just write it. Write it on receipts in the car while you wait for your kids to finish their piano lessons, scribble on napkins at lunch with friends. Type on crappy typewriters or borrow computers if you have to. Fill notebooks with ink. Write inside your head while you're in traffic and when you're sitting in the doctor's office. Write your dreams. Write your nightmares. Write while you cry about what you're writing, write while you laugh out loud at your own words... be brave. Just write."

—Melodie Ramone, author of *After Forever Ends*

When we start looking at *how* we write and the different approaches, practices, and obstacles we may experience within a given day, I find that talking about writing leads to talking about *endurance*. How do we keep going through life's daily demands and challenges, as well as the imposter syndrome and other limiting beliefs that may sometimes stop us in our tracks?

The reality is sitting down every day and hitting our writing targets uninterrupted, all the while receiving a continuous stream of inspiration and knowing what part comes next, is absolutely achievable, but our lives and the nature of writing are much more variable and textured. We need to be flexible, creative, and solutions-focused in how we approach the task of actually writing a book. What works for some doesn't always work for others. This chapter will provide a variety of ways to help you go the distance.

Demystifying the writing process is a good place to start, as it's likely you have adopted beliefs about writing that are either untrue or not applicable to you. To think you must spend years writing a book is an illusion—a book can actually be written in 30 days! If the average business book is 158 pages long, comprised of 37,000 words, at an average of 235 words on each page, then that amounts to 1,250 words per day for 30 days, which is entirely doable. One chapter per day is even better. You can even speak your book into print by using a recording and/or transcribing app on your phone. That's five pages a day or 10 minutes of daily recording and *Hey, presto!* Your first draft is ready for review.

Many writers speak of "writer's block," being time-poor, and feeling isolated while on the job—all common culprits (or perhaps excuses?) for not quite finishing the final manuscript. Yet when we explore the different methods of writing with the following tips and ideas, as well as setting markers to hold you accountable to finishing projects, I can guarantee your writing journey will be very different.

Going on writing retreats, doing a writing course, joining groups, or hiring a mentor are some of the ways you can support yourself to keep going and developing your manuscript. You may not have even considered some of the ideas I'm presenting; however, please view them as suggested tools for your writing toolbox. Every author needs tricks of the trade up their sleeves! And remember that having fun and finding suitable methods also increases the likelihood of you achieving your desired outcomes. Do what works for you, and you'll enjoy the process so much you won't even notice the time it's taken.

Top Tips for Writing a Book

1. A writer writes. If you want to be a writer, write.

2. Use simple sentences. Write as if you were speaking to a good friend.

3. Never start at Chapter 1. You'll get stage fright. Start writing the easiest chapter first.

4. Don't edit—just write! Just get the words down. Don't worry about grammar, punctuation, or style. Keep writing in bursts of 30–45 minutes. Then take a 10-minute break.

5. Block out an appointment with yourself to write each day or each week. Momentum leads to completion of your book.

6. Read or listen to books in your genre/category.

7. Always reference words and ideas you have found in other people's books. Otherwise, it's considered plagiarism. A good rule is never to copy three words in a row from any other book.

8. Layer your work in your nonfiction book—start with a story (people love reading stories), and then discuss it in a way that's relevant to your reader. Follow this with an interesting statistic or

fact. Then discuss. That way, you're using a variety of techniques to keep the subject matter interesting, and your reader remains engaged.

9. In your nonfiction book, use lots of real-life and personal stories, case studies, facts, checklists, quizzes, pull quotes, expert opinions, bullet points, sidebars, breakout boxes, etc. to make it interesting to read.

10. Write the date and source of your quotes. Immediately contact necessary sources for permission. Keep all documentation even after your book has been published. See pages 82–86 for more details.

11. There is no such thing as writer's block! If you are waiting for inspiration, you'll be waiting a long time. Use the 10-minute rule: sit down at your desk and start writing for 10 minutes. If you still don't feel like writing after that, you have permission to leave. This is doubtful, though—as most likely, by then you'll be into it.

12. Still procrastinating about writing your book? One of the best ways to unblock yourself is to buy or borrow a copy of *The Artist's Way* by Julia Cameron and start writing your Morning Pages every day. This practice is life-changing; it will unleash your creativity and get you into a state of flow in just a few days. You could also find a book coach to help you set some writing deadlines and who will hold you accountable. Or collaborate with a friend or an expert as a coauthor. Or find a specialist writer in your genre who is a ghostwriter to assist you. You can find a copywriter or ghostwriter on Upwork.com*. Here is the link: https://upwork.pxf.io/c/347458/1062918/13634 (See how to post a job on Upwork* on page 156).

Your Ideal Day as a Writer

What would you do in your ideal day as a writer? This is a powerful tool for living more consciously because it helps focus you on what you really want to be doing with your time versus what you are currently doing. It's about finding the pockets of time in our day and week that we can devote to writing and working on our books rather than mindlessly scrolling social media or watching TV.

Below is an example of an author's daily plan. Your day may look different from the one below. You may have an incredibly busy full-time job and a family to take care of. But trust me, there is also space to write. For example, before I had my children, I'd spend Sundays writing at the library. Now that I have a full-time business and a family, I go to bed earlier and wake at 5:00 a.m. to write before the kids wake up at 6:00 a.m. The bliss I experience from being able to write each day is priceless. Remember, it's about organizing your life to make your dreams a priority.

"Talent is insignificant. I know a lot of talented ruins. Beyond talent lie all the usual words: discipline, love, luck, but most of all, endurance."

—James Baldwin, author of *Go Tell It on the Mountain*

Have a look at this example, then create your own below.

6:30 a.m.	Wake up and meditate for 15 minutes. Make myself a coffee and do my three Morning Pages from *The Artist's Way* by Julia Cameron to get the creative juices flowing.
7:00 a.m.	Take the dog for a walk and listen to inspiring music and podcasts to enhance creativity.
7:30 a.m.	Shower and get ready. Have breakfast—a glass of green juice, plus oatmeal with fruit.
8:30 a.m.	Spend one hour writing my book while listening to uplifting music from award-winning movies.
9:30 a.m.	Start work from home.
12:30 p.m.	Zoom session with someone I'm interviewing for my book.
1:00 p.m.	Send off my interview recording to be transcribed through Fiverr.com* or Upwork.com*. (Fiverr.com* and Upwork.com* are websites where you can hire freelancers for a wide range of services.)
5:30 p.m.	Finish work for the day.
6:00 p.m.	Go for a walk or do some yoga to clear my head.
7:30 p.m.	Do some housework and prepare a healthy dinner.
8:00 p.m.	Spend time with my partner.
9:00 p.m.	Read one of my favorite authors.
9:30 p.m.	Write a list of the top three things to do tomorrow and five things I have accomplished today.
10:00 p.m.	Sleep and dream about being a successful author.

MY IDEAL DAY AS A WRITER

Time a.m./p.m.   Activity

_____

_____

_____

_____

_____

_____

_____

_____

_____

_____

_____

_____

_____

_____

_____

_____

_____

_____

Start incorporating some of these activities into your daily life.

WHEN CAN I MAKE SPACE IN MY WEEK TO WRITE?

Next week   Writing time

MONDAY

TUESDAY

WEDNESDAY

THURSDAY

FRIDAY

SATURDAY

SUNDAY

When Do You Want to Complete Writing Your Manuscript?

I want to finish my manuscript by _____ .

I will devote _____ hours a day/week until I've finished my manuscript.

I am committed to writing _____ words a day/week until I have finished my manuscript.

What will you need to give up in order to achieve your goal of writing your book?

Examples:

1. *Watching TV two nights a week.*

2. *Scrolling on social media.*

3. *Reading the news.*

4. *Sunday afternoons socializing with friends.*

5. *Aimlessly surfing the internet.*

What I will give up in order to achieve my goal:

1. _____

2. _____

3. _____

4. _____

5. _____

What habits do you need to implement to ensure your goal is completed by the due date?

Examples:

1. I need to block out two to three hours every Sunday afternoon.

2. I need to go to the library to ensure I have no distractions.

1. _____

2. _____

3. _____

4. _____

5. _____

What support do you need to reach your goal?

_____

_____

_____

_____

_____

_____

_____

_____

_____

_____

_____

_____

WRITING SPACE

What does your writing space look like? Every writer needs a writing space free of clutter that inspires them, supports their writing, and encourages productivity. Does your writing space support you?

Yes ☐ No ☐

If *yes*, well done! You're on the right track. If *no*, what can you do to ensure it is a supportive, creative space?

_____

_____

_____

_____

_____

_____

If you are too easily distracted at home, go to the library or find a quiet café that supports your writing goals.

The place I will go to write my book is:

_____

_____

_____

_____

_____

_____

WRITING RETREAT

If you need to take yourself away from daily life for an extended period, why not book a writing holiday somewhere? A house in the country? A week's holiday by the beach?

I will organize a writing holiday in _____ for _____ days/weeks.

WRITING TOOLS

Do you have the correct writing tools? Which of the following writing tools do you have?

It doesn't matter whether you are handwriting your book, typing your book, or recording your book. What matters is that the way you do it works for you.

- [ ] Pen and paper
- [ ] Word
- [ ] Google Docs
- [ ] PC
- [ ] Mac
- [ ] Pad with keypad
- [ ] Scrivener software for authors
- [ ] Voice-to-text app to dictate your book

Note: To write my books, I use Word, as it is hard to beat for features and convenience. Most professional editors prefer to edit your manuscript in Word using the *track changes* tool. Furthermore, book formatters will find it easy to ensure a smooth conversion into the book publishing software InDesign, if you have a Word manuscript that is correctly formatted with paragraphs, headings, references, footnotes, and hyperlinks. The book template I give you in the next section is in Word, so it will be easy for you to cut and paste your own document into this template.

Having said that, I handwrote this book because typing felt too much like being "at work," and I wanted to engage my creativity through handwriting. Once I'd finished, I quickly typed it into Word. So, choose whatever works for you to get your book done, then type it or get it typed into a Word document so you can use my book template and make it easy for the editor and typesetter who formats your book. You can download my book template at iinspiremedia.com.au.

CAN I USE AI TO WRITE A BOOK?

The answer is yes, you can. You can ask apps like ChatGPT to write you a novel, nonfiction book, or children's book, and it will churn out an incredibly well-worded book in a few seconds!

In my opinion, using AI to write a book does not make you an author. Writing a book is a journey. It takes dedication to carve time out of your everyday life, research your subject, and craft the words you want to use. It takes courage and resilience to overcome imposter syndrome and writer's block along the way. And it takes patience to keep at it until you've finally hit the publish button. Nothing beats the joy and sense of accomplishment when you are holding your hard work in your hand.

Holding a published book that you knew was generated by AI would be cheating, not only cheating you of the experience of becoming an author but cheating others who believed that you achieved it in the same way others had.

The biggest issue for using AI is that we have no idea where the text for your book is coming from. It is likely being pulled from existing books and articles that have already been published on the internet, which means you have essentially plagiarized other people's work.

AI-generated books are flooding Amazon to the point where Amazon is now limiting authors to self-publishing three books a day. Amazon currently does not prohibit the use of AI, but Kindle Direct Publishing now requires you to inform them of AI-generated content (text, interior and exterior images, or translations) by ticking a box when you publish.

KDP also states that if you created the content yourself but used AI-based tools to edit, refine, error-check, or otherwise improve that content, then it is considered AI-assisted and not AI-generated, and it is not necessary to inform them of the use of these tools or processes.

My advice is if you are using AI to create books, proceed with caution. Amazon KDP states that they currently "use a combination of machine learning, automation, and dedicated teams of human reviewers to detect and remove content that does not adhere to content guidelines." Amazon KDP has strict policies regarding content quality and originality. These require authors to provide original works that do not infringe copyright or intellectual property rights. If the AI-generated content you publish does not meet these standards, your account may be suspended or terminated. I have witnessed instances of Amazon simply shutting down author accounts and these authors spending months desperately trying to get their accounts back to no avail.

At this stage, if you plan on publishing on Amazon, I recommend ensuring that no part of your book is generated with AI so you can avoid the risk of having your book removed from publication and your account suspended for good.

Just for the record, none of this book was generated or assisted using AI.

"I would like to be remembered as someone who did the best she could with the talent she had."

—J. K. Rowling, author of the Harry Potter series

Surround Yourself with Successful Writers

Attending writer's workshops where you can hone your craft with the help of a writing teacher, or getting specific feedback from a writing mentor in your genre can be so helpful. You can also do some fantastic online writing courses on Udemy.com. Attending a writer's support group will give you the opportunity to bounce ideas off other writers and get constructive feedback on your writing. And an accountability buddy will hold you to your writing goals.

WRITING COURSE	Have you done a short writing course to improve your writing skills?	Yes ☐ No ☐
WRITING GROUP	Do you have a writers' support group where you can receive encouragement and honest feedback on your writing?	Yes ☐ No ☐
WRITING MENTOR	Do you have a writing mentor who can support your genre of writing (romance, crime, fantasy, etc.)?	Yes ☐ No ☐

If you had your choice of mentor in your genre, who would it be? E.g., Say you are a crime fiction writer. Your top three crime fiction writers by whom you'd love to be mentored might be Stephen King, Michael Connelly, and Stieg Larsson. Write those names down.

Choice 1: _____

Choice 2. _____

Choice 3. _____

Why don't you contact them and ask? They may be flattered and say *yes*!

ACCOUNTABILITY BUDDY

Do you have a best friend, family member, or fellow writer who can hold you accountable for achieving your writing goals?

My accountability buddy is _____ .

I want to finish my manuscript by _____ .

MUSIC THAT HELPS YOU WRITE

Music transports you to another dimension. Maximize your writing focus by playing classical, ambient, jazz, or movie soundtracks. What music enhances your writing experience?

1. _____

2. _____

3. _____

READ TO IMPROVE

Read as much in your genre and subgenre as you can, either *prior to* or *during the course of* writing your book. For example, if you are writing a historical romance novel, read historical romance novels set in the same time period to help you hone your skills and master your craft. If you have limited time to read, then listen to audiobooks while you are cleaning, driving, and shopping.

The next three books in my genre I'm going to read are:

1. _____

2. _____

3. _____

What Actions Will You Need to Finish Your Book by Your Due Date?

Example Actions:

1. *I need to interview 9–10 parents of deaf and hard-of-hearing children and record their personal stories.*
2. *I need to interview five experts in the field of hearing loss and record their expert opinions.*
3. *I need to have my interviews transcribed by someone on Fiverr.com* or Upwork.com*.*
4. *I need to write seven chapters in seven weeks.*

My Actions:

1. _____
2. _____
3. _____
4. _____

Your Motivational Tool Kit

When you are feeling deflated and unmotivated, have a list of go-to actions you can do to lift your spirits and energize you.

Examples:

1. *Watch two to three inspirational videos on YouTube.*
2. *Go for a walk in nature and appreciate the beauty and simplicity in your life.*
3. *Have a massage or a pampering session.*
4. *Take a bath with candles.*
5. *Chat with a good friend.*

When I'm feeling deflated, I will:

1. _____

2. _____

3. _____

4. _____

5. _____

Self-Publishing Success Story —Kim McCosker and Rachel Bermingham

Australian mums and lifelong friends, Kim McCosker and Rachel Birmingham wrote the cookbook *4 Ingredients* together in 2007 and then tried to get it published, but no mainstream publisher would touch it; they said it was boring and had no pictures. So, they decided to self-publish 2,000 copies of the book and sell it themselves. It became Australia's bestselling nonfiction book that year. Since then, they have become the highest-selling authors in Australian history. This book, as well as their other *4 Ingredients* titles, have gone on to sell close to 9 million combined copies. They filmed their own TV show, *4 Ingredients*, which aired on the Lifestyle Channel in 23 countries. They also launched a cooking app and a cookware range. As Kim said, "No one is more surprised than us!" (Booktopia 2020).

I cannot wait to read some of the books that will be produced by working through this workbook!

Make sure you join my Facebook group, *Heart-Centred Authors (Writing, Self-Publishing and Marketing Books)*. Share your thoughts and ideas, and get support and feedback for your title, subtitle, and writing from others in the community. I look forward to seeing you there!

"If there's a book that you want to read, but it hasn't been written yet, then you must write it."

—Toni Morrison, author of 11 novels including *Song of Solomon* and *Beloved*

Completing Your Book Template

You've finished writing your book in whatever way you've chosen to create it, and you've transferred it to a Word document that is correctly formatted with paragraphs, headings, references, footnotes, and hyperlinks. Now it's time to make your manuscript look like an actual book.

Go to iinspiremedia.com.au

and download your book template—there are separate ones for nonfiction books, fiction books, and children's books in Word. Open the book template and "Save As" your Book Title into a folder on your desktop. Then adapt the template for your own book. Have a look at books in your genre to see how they are laid out and follow a similar path.

Title

Insert your short, catchy two- or three-word working title, e.g., *Burnout*. Ideally your title should contain your main keyword/s and eliminate all confusion around what your book is about. If it doesn't, put your keyword/s in the subtitle.

_____

_____

_____

_____

_____

_____

Subtitle

Insert your working subtitle containing the keywords of your nonfiction book, e.g., *The Secret to Unlocking the Stress Cycle*.

It used to be that fiction books and children's books didn't have a subtitle, but now more and more books have one so that they rank well on Amazon's search engine, e.g., *The Family Across the Street: A Totally Unputdownable Psychological Thriller with a Shocking Twist*. Or *Kindness Is My Superpower: A Children's Book About Empathy, Kindness, and Compassion*.

Amazon states that together, your title and subtitle must be 200 characters or less, and that the title and the subtitle on your cover need to match what you put in the metadata on the IngramSpark and Kindle Direct Publishing platforms and vice versa—refer to the *Publish* chapter for more information.

_____

_____

_____

Praise Page

How do you get praise for your book before it has even been published? Ask for it! When you send your book out to your 5–10 beta readers, ask them for a testimonial at the same time.

You could also send a chapter or the entire manuscript to various experts in that field, or colleagues, peers, organizations or even friends and ask them to read the chapter or manuscript and give you a testimonial. As most people are time-poor, you may even offer to write something for them that they can change to make their own. It's so much easier to edit something than write it from scratch.

What Are Beta Readers?

Your beta readers are a trusted group of people you know who will give you honest, specific feedback about your book and save you a lot of poor reviews on Amazon down the line. Think of them as your test readers. (See *Editing* in the next section.)

When the beta readers return their feedback, it should have the person's first name and last name as well as their job title or something that gives them credibility, such as:

"This is the best book I have read about sustainability." —John James, CEO of Electric Publishing *or* —John James, author of *Everything You Need to Know about Electricity.*

Who can you ask to write you a testimonial?

1. _____

2. _____

3. _____

Imprint Page

Every book has an imprint page that gives you all the important information about your book—who wrote it, who published it, where the book was printed, what the ISBNs are, etc. Everything you need to put on your imprint page is on the book template. This includes who published the book (your publishing business name), the copyright notice, the "All Rights Reserved" copyright statement, your book's International Standard Book Number (ISBN), the National Library Cataloguing Statement (or Library of Congress Control Number in the US), any disclaimers, the name of the editor who performed editing services, the name of the graphic designer/s who designed your cover and book layout, and the name of the printer.

EXAMPLE OF AN IMPRINT PAGE

Published in Australia by
iinspire media
Melbourne, Australia
info@iinspiremedia.com.au
www.iinspiremedia.com.au

First published in Australia 2024
Copyright © Julie Postance 2023

All rights reserved. No part of this publication may be reproduced, stored in a retrieval system, or transmitted in any form or by any means without the prior written permission of the publisher, nor be otherwise circulated in any form of binding or cover other than that in which it is published and without a similar condition being imposed on the subsequent purchaser.

National Library of Australia Cataloguing in Publication entry

A catalogue record for this book is available from the National Library of Australia

Postance, Julie

The Self-Publishing Workbook: The Life-Changing Guide to Writing, Publishing, and Marketing
Your Book, Becoming a Bestselling Author, and Making an Impact

ISBN: 978-0-9805953-4-5 (paperback)
ISBN: 978-0-9805953-5-2 (hardback)
ISBN: 978-0-9805953-6-9 (e-book)

Edited for US publication by Cortni L. Merritt
Cover design by Aleaca
Layout by Sophie White Design
Printed by IngramSpark

All care has been taken in the preparation of the information herein, but no responsibility can be accepted by the publisher or author for errors, omissions, or contrary interpretations on the subject matter. All details given in this book were current at the time of publication but are subject to change.

This book is for informational purposes only. The advice given in this book is based on the experience of the author. No guarantees for earnings or any other results of any kind are being made by the author or publisher, nor are any liabilities being assumed. The reader is entirely responsible for his or her actions. The author and publisher shall not be responsible for any person with regard to any loss or damage caused directly or indirectly by the information in this book. Professionals should be consulted for individual issues.

Figure 5. Imprint page of *The Self-Publishing Workbook*, published 2024.

Let's break this down.

YOUR PUBLISHING BUSINESS NAME

If you don't want your book to look self-published, it's a good idea to create a professional-sounding publishing business name that makes you look like you have been published by a mainstream publishing company, e.g., Integrity Media, Integrity Press, Integrity Books, or Integrity Publishing. Please don't use your own name as part of the business name.

The name needs to be short—one or two words—and resonate with you and your brand. It can be followed by Media, Press, Books, or Publishing.

You will need to research the name to make sure it's not already in use before you start using it. Registering a business name is relatively easy and inexpensive to do.

If you are in the US, go to: sba.gov/business-guide/launch-your-business/choose-your-business-name

If you are in Canada, go to: canada.ca/en/services/business/start/choosing-a-business-name-3.html

If you are in Australia, go to: asic.gov.au/for-business/registering-a-business-name/

If you are in the UK, go to: gov.uk/set-up-sole-trader

Before you register the name, talk with your accountant about which business structure is best for you and your publishing business. Many self-publishing authors choose to be a sole proprietor, sole trader, or individual, which is the easiest type of business to form.

Later, you'll need to have a simple logo designed to go on the back cover and spine of your book. There are plenty of talented logo designers on Fiverr.com*, for example, and it can cost as little as

US$10. Here is the link: https://fvrr.co/2SxlAAV. Please don't worry about creating a website for your publishing name unless you want a whole lot of people contacting you about publishing their books!

My publishing business name ideas are:

1. _____

2. _____

3. _____

YOUR AUTHOR WEBSITE DOMAIN

Please secure the following domain names for your author website:

1. FirstNameSurname.com (e.g., www.kellyparsons.com)

2. If your author name is already taken, then add "author" to the domain name (i.e., www.kellyparsonsauthor.com). If you have more than one book, you could also use "books" at the end—www.kellyparsonsbooks.com.

3. BookTitle.com (e.g., www.opshopulence.com)

4. Subject-Oriented Domain Names (e.g., www.communitychange.com.au)

This is a good idea if you are writing a nonfiction book, and you're going to become an expert in that field. If you know your keywords, try to use a domain name containing keywords that are frequently going to be typed into search engines.

You can register your domain names at a domain company such as Godaddy.com. They cost less than US$20 a year. You aren't limited to one domain name, and you can ask your web developer to redirect your domains to one author website. (See more on author websites in the *Promote* chapter.)

YOUR COPYRIGHT DATE

Ideas, facts, and titles are not protectable by copyright. You could, however, trademark your title for a series of books (e.g., Chicken Soup for the Soul) through a lawyer if you wish since it serves the role of a brand. Your actual manuscript will be copyrighted as soon as it is in written form. In Australia and the UK, there is no copyright registration process. However, in the US, it is advised to register your manuscript with the US Copyright Office at Copyright.gov for a fee of US$45.

Putting a copyright notice on your manuscript is helpful to remind people that the work is protected by copyright. It also lets people know who is claiming copyright and is the presumed copyright owner. Put the copyright symbol plus your name and the year you published, i.e., © 2024 Your Name on the imprint page of your manuscript like this:

First published in Australia 2024
Copyright © Julie Postance 2024

Copyright lasts for the term of the author's life plus 50–70 years (depending on the copyright law of that country). Please refer to pages 82–86 for more information.

ALL RIGHTS RESERVED CLAUSE

Make sure you have the following clause on your imprint page—it just means that no one can copy or reproduce your book without asking you first:

All rights reserved. No part of this publication may be reproduced, stored in a retrieval system, or transmitted, in any form or by any means without the prior written permission of the publisher, nor be otherwise circulated in any form of binding or cover other than that in which it is published and without a similar condition being imposed on the subsequent purchaser.

CATALOGUING STATEMENT

A cataloguing statement is a bibliographic record prepared by the National Library of Australia and has replaced CiP entries for publishers to print in their books. This is an optional extra, but it's free, and it means the details of your book will be made available to libraries, library suppliers, and other members of the book industry for acquisition purposes.

In Australia, you can apply to be added here: nla.gov.au/content/prepublication-data-service.

You can download a cataloguing statement from nla.gov.au/cataloguing-statement with a logo, which you can include on your imprint page before it is published. It looks like this:

A catalogue record for this book is available from the National Library of Australia

Applications are now processed instantly, eliminating the old 10-day timeframe. Once you receive your email confirmation, the process is complete.

When your book is published, you will receive an email from the National Library requesting a copy for their records. You are legally required to deposit or deliver your book within one month of publication. If both formats are available, your electronic version is preferred, and you can deposit an ePub version of your book via the National eDeposit service.

If you are in the US, you need to apply for an LCCN Number from the US Library of Congress. Follow the instructions from the website of the US Library of Congress. Once you receive your LCCN number, then place it on the imprint page of your book. Mail a copy of your book to the Library of Congress.

For Canada: library-archives.canada.ca/eng/services/publishers/cataloguing-publication/Pages/cataloguing-publication.aspx

For the UK: bdslive.com/publishers/upload-your-metadata/

ISBN

ISBN stands for *International Standard Book Number*. It is a unique number to identify your book around the world.

Using ISBNs allows you to better manage your book's metadata and ensure maximum discoverability of your book. Your book will then be listed in Bowker Books in Print®, which is used by all the major search engines and most bookstores and libraries.

To buy your ISBNs in various locations visit the following URLs:

US: myidentifiers.com/identify-protect-your-book/isbn/buy-isbn

Canada: library-archives.canada.ca/eng

UK: nielsenisbnstore.com/Home/Isbn

Australia: myidentifiers.com.au/identify-protect-your-book/isbn/buy-isbn

The ISBN will be included on the imprint page of your book and on the back cover just above the barcode. You will need to register as a new publisher, then purchase a single ISBN or a bundle of 10.

It's a good idea to buy the bundle of 10 because you will need separate ISBNs for the different versions of your book (paperback, hardback, e-book, and audiobook). Ideally you will use the same ISBN for the paperback versions that you publish on IngramSpark and Kindle Direct Publishing to create one listing on Amazon. However, you may get rejected by one or the other platform for using the same ISBN (an error message may come up saying, "This ISBN is already in use"). To prevent this from happening, I often use two different ISBNs when publishing a paperback on IngramSpark and KDP. Please see the *Publish* chapter.

You will not need one for your e-book on Kindle Direct Publishing as you will receive an Amazon Standard Book Number (ASIN).

However, if you decide to publish your ePub to IngramSpark down the road, or upload your ePub to the National Deposit, then they require an ISBN, so keep one on file. Also, you may decide to do a special custom-made paperback or hardback through a specialist printer. In this case, use a different ISBN.

MY 10 ISBNS

1. ___ _ _____ _ _ (IngramSpark paperback)

2. ___ _ _____ _ _ (IngramSpark hardback)

3. ___ _ _____ _ _ (ePub)

4. ___ _ _____ _ _ (KDP paperback)

5. ___ _ _____ _ _ (Audiobook version)

6. ___ _ _____ _ _ (Special printer)

Leave remaining ISBNs for your future books. They never expire.

7. ___ _ _____ _ _

8. ___ _ _____ _ _

9. ___ _ _____ _ _

10. ___ _ _____ _ _

DISCLAIMER

Here are some examples of disclaimers. Find a book that most resembles your book and adapt the disclaimer for your book. For a more comprehensive list of disclaimers, visit my website iinspiremedia.com.au/disclaimers.

1. Some names and identifying details have been changed to protect the privacy of individuals. (memoir, recent history)

2. This is a work of fiction. Names, characters, businesses, places, events, and incidents are either the products of the author's imagination or used in a fictitious manner. Any resemblance to actual persons living or dead or actual events is purely coincidental. (novels, short stories)

3. Although the author and publisher have made every effort to ensure that the information in this book was correct at press time, the author and publisher do not assume and hereby disclaim any liability to any party for any loss, damage, or disruption caused by errors or omissions, whether such errors or omissions result from negligence, accident, or any other cause. (advice, how-to)

My disclaimer will be:

_____

_____

_____

_____

About the Author Page

If you have a nonfiction book, you will have a short author bio on the back cover and a longer About the Author page either at the front or the back of the book. If you are writing fiction, a short About the Author section usually goes at the back of a book. A children's book doesn't have an author bio, but you'll need one to put on your Amazon Author page. Have a look at recent books in your genre to see where the author information is placed. An About the Author section is always written in the third person ("he", "she" or "they", not "I").

ABOUT THE AUTHOR BIO

Here are items to consider including in your bio:

☐ Professional background

☐ Education

☐ Current business or profession

☐ Achievements or awards

☐ Previous publishing experience

☐ Personal details (family, city of residence, personal interests, etc.)

☐ Contact information (you want readers to reach out to you, right?) Include your website URL.

☐ If it's a nonfiction book and you choose to use a photo of yourself, please use a professional photo (please, please, please don't crop yourself out of a group photo or use something that looks unprofessional!)

If you can, demonstrate any relevant authority and professional standing on your book's subject. Include anything that builds credibility or is interesting. Mention any books you have previously written and your website. If you don't have any relevant qualifications or experience and no previously published books, don't worry! Mention anything quirky or authentic to which readers can relate.

EXAMPLE OF A SHORT AUTHOR BIO ON THE BACK COVER OF A NONFICTION BOOK

The following short author bio is taken from the back cover of *Wabi Sabi Love: The Ancient Art of Finding Perfect Love in Imperfect Relationships* by Arielle Ford.

Arielle Ford is an acclaimed relationship expert and the international bestselling author of *The Soulmate Secret*. Visit the author online at www.wabisabilove.com.

EXAMPLE OF A LONG ABOUT THE AUTHOR BIO ON THE INSIDE FRONT OR BACK OF A NONFICTION BOOK

The longer About the Author bio below can be found on the inside back page of *Wabi Sabi Love: The Ancient Art of Finding Perfect Love in Imperfect Relationships* by Arielle Ford:

Arielle Ford is a leading personality in the personal growth and contemporary spirituality movement. For the past twenty-five years she has been living, teaching, and promoting consciousness through all forms of media. Her stellar career includes years as a prominent book publicist, author, literary agent, TV lifestyle reporter, television producer, Sirius radio host, publishing consultant, relationship expert, speaker, columnist, and blogger for the Huffington Post.

Arielle is a gifted writer and the author of eight books including the international bestseller *The Soulmate Secret: Manifest the Love of Your Life with the Law of Attraction*. She has been called the "Cupid of Consciousness" and the "Fairy Godmother of Love" and believes that with a simple Wabi Sabi shift in perception, couples can discover the beauty and perfection in themselves and their partners, leading to a deeper, more loving, and more fulfilling relationship.

She lives in La Jolla, California, with her husband/soulmate Brian Hilliard, and their feline friends. www.arielleford.com

My short author bio for the back cover of my nonfiction book is:

_____

_____

_____

_____

_____

_____

_____

_____

My long About the Author bio for the inside back or front of my nonfiction book is:

_____

_____

_____

_____

_____

_____

EXAMPLE OF A SHORT ABOUT THE AUTHOR BIO ON THE BACK INSIDE PAGE OF A FICTION BOOK

The following bio can be found on the back inside page of *Memoirs of a Geisha* by Arthur Golden (Vintage 1998).

Arthur Golden was born and brought up in Chattanooga, Tennessee. He is a 1978 graduate of Harvard College with a degree in art history, specializing in Japanese art. In 1980, he earned an MA in Japanese history from Columbia University, where he also learned Mandarin Chinese. After a summer at Beijing University, he went to work at a magazine in Tokyo. In 1988, he received an MA in English from Boston University. He has lived and worked in Japan, and since that time has been teaching writing and literature in the Boston area. He now lives in Brookline, Massachusetts, with his wife and children.

My short author bio for the inside back cover of my fiction book is:

_____

_____

_____

_____

_____

_____

_____

_____

Acknowledgments Page

This is a great opportunity to formally thank all of those who have helped you in the amazing feat of publishing a book. I would advise placing your Acknowledgments page at the back of your book. Never forget it took a village to create your book—it is not a lone activity. Remember to thank everyone who helped in the process, including your family and friends who provided their emotional support.

EXAMPLE OF AN ACKNOWLEDGMENTS PAGE

This Acknowledgments page can be found in the back of Lisa Shea's first 10 medieval romance novels including *Knowing Yourself, Finding Peace, A Sense of Duty,* and *Trusting in Faith.*

Thanks to:

My mom, dad, and siblings, who encouraged me to indulge in my medieval fantasies. I spent many long car rides creating epic tales of sword-wielding heroines and the strong men who stood by their sides.

Jody, Leslie, and Sarah, my childhood friends, who enjoy my eclectic ways and provide great suggestions.

Peter and Elizabeth May, who patiently toured me around England, Scotland, and France on three separate occasions.

The editors at BellaOnline, who inspire me daily to reach for my dreams and to aim for the stars. Lisa, Cheryll, Jeanne, Lizzie, Moe, and Terrie provided insightful feedback to help my polishing efforts.

The Mensa Writing Group for their feedback and enthusiastic support. Lynn and Dean both offered great advice!

Academy of Knightly Arts for several years of in-depth training and combat experience with medieval swords and knives.

B&R Stables, who renewed my love of horseback riding.

My son, James, whose insights into psychology help ground my characters in authentic behavior.

Bob See, my partner in love for over 20 years and counting. He enthusiastically supports all my new projects.

My Acknowledgments page will say:

_____

_____

_____

_____

_____

_____

_____

_____

_____

_____

_____

Dedication

To whom are you going to dedicate your book?

EXAMPLES OF DEDICATIONS

Ally Condie, *Matched*

For Scott, who always believes.

Carl Sagan, *Cosmos: The Story of Cosmic Evolution, Science and Civilisation*

In the vastness of space and immensity of time, it is my joy to spend a planet and an epoch with Annie.

My Dedication will say:

_____

_____

_____

_____

_____

_____

_____

_____

Content Warning or Trigger Warning

Content warnings or trigger warnings are becoming more common in both nonfiction and fiction books to alert readers that the book contains sensitive themes, scenes, or subjects that could be potentially upsetting for the reader. Subjects that you may wish to warn your readers about include, but are not limited to rape, sexual abuse, child abuse, violence, racism, death of a parent or child, violence, suicide, and drug addiction. If your book contains potentially triggering material, you may wish to include a "Note to the Reader" on one of the front pages of your book.

EXAMPLES OF CONTENT WARNINGS/TRIGGER WARNINGS

T. J. Klune, *Under the Whispering Door*

This story explores life and love as well as loss and grief. There are discussions of death in different forms—quiet, unexpected, and death by suicide. Please read with care.

Zane Riley, *When It's Time*

This book contains recurring discussions of past sexual assault.

My Content Warning will say:

_____

_____

_____

Contents Page

You will most definitely have one in a nonfiction book, but most novels and memoirs do not have a contents page. It's time to take the content ideas of your mind map and turn them into chapter headings for your nonfiction book. Choose a single word or a few words that tell your readers what the chapter is about and then craft them into engaging, juicy, irresistible chapter headings. You can turn to the internet for inspiration if you get stuck.

YOUR CONTENTS PAGE

Chapter Number	Boring Heading	New Enticing Heading
Example: Chapter 1	*Being a Leader*	*So, You Want to Be a #Girlboss?*

Foreword

You will only find a Foreword in a nonfiction book. It is usually written by a well-known or important expert in the field who is prepared to introduce and praise your book. Don't be afraid to dream big! Who would you ask if you knew you couldn't fail? Tracey Stranger, author of *How to Overcome Stress Naturally*, asked His Holiness the Dalai Lama to write her Foreword, and he agreed! Consider contacting a celebrity or a top expert in your genre who could really add credibility to your book.

Who would you love to ask?

The top three people I'd love to ask to write the Foreword to my book:

1. _____

2. _____

3. _____

Introduction

You will usually find an Introduction at the beginning of a nonfiction book. This is written by *you,* and I would recommend writing it last. This is where you tell people why you are writing your book, why you're qualified to write this book, what is contained in your book, and what people are going to gain by reading it (the benefits). Read some examples in various nonfiction books in your genre before you write yours.

My Introduction is:

_____

_____

_____

_____

_____

_____

_____

_____

_____

_____

_____

_____

_____

_____

_____

_____

_____

_____

_____

Bibliography or References

Always acknowledge the books you used in a nonfiction book to avoid being accused of plagiarism. The References is a list of all the sources you have cited in your book, including books, e-books, articles, and websites.

A Bibliography is a list of references you have cited in your work plus other background readings you have read in researching for the book.

Creating a Reference List

Creating a Reference list at the back of your book is a difficult task, even for professional editors, as there are so many rules to follow within the style guide that you choose. My advice is just to do your best to include as much information as possible, and then pay an editor to finalize it.

If you are using US English, then the *Chicago Manual of Style,* 18th edition (CMOS) is probably the most-used style guide for fiction and nonfiction books in the United States. In Canada, the predominant style guide is *The Canadian Style: A Guide to Writing and Editing*. If you are using UK English, then the preferred style guide is the *New Oxford Style Manual*. And if you are using Australian English, the *Style Manual for Authors, Editors and Printers,* 6th edition, published by John Wiley & Sons is the recommended style guide for most publishing companies in Australia.

If you are using US English, then your editor will use referencing from the US *Chicago Manual of Style*. Examples of referencing a book, journal article or website according to CMOS are shown below.

Referencing a Book

STRUCTURE

First Author Surname, First Name, and Second Author First Name Surname. Year published. *Title of Book: Subtitle of Book.* City of Publication: Publisher.

EXAMPLE

Grazer, Brian, and Charles Fishman. 2015. *A Curious Mind: The Secret to a Bigger Life.* New York: Simon & Schuster.

Referencing a Journal Article

STRUCTURE

Author Surname, First Name, Second Author First Name Last Name, and Third Author First Name Last Name. Year. "Article Title: Article Subtitle." *Journal Title*, Volume Number, no. Issue Number (Month): page–page. DOI.

EXAMPLE

Satterfield, Susan. 2016. "Livy and the *Pax Deum*." *Classical Philology* 111, no. 2 (April): 165–76.

Referencing a Website

STRUCTURE

Author Surname/Organization, First Name. Year. "Title of the Article/Webpage." Website Name. Accessed Month Day, Year. URL.

EXAMPLE

Yale University. 2020. "About Yale: Yale Facts." Accessed May 1, 2020. https://www.yale.edu/about-yale/yale-facts.

Useful Contacts

If you have written a book about mental health issues, for example, you could list all the mental health organizations, books, websites, and newsletters that your readers and their families may find beneficial. Another benefit is that these organizations are more likely to promote your book to their networks if they have been mentioned in your book.

USEFUL CONTACTS

Suicide and Crisis Lifeline
Text or call: 988
988lifeline.org
Anyone experiencing a personal crisis or thinking about suicide.
Free and confidential.
Available 24/7
English and Spanish available.

National Domestic Violence Hotline
Call: 800-799-7233
English, Spanish, & 200+ languages through interpretation service
thehotline.org
Available 24/7

MY USEFUL CONTACTS

List some of the useful resources (organizations, websites, and books) you could mention in the back of your nonfiction book.

_____

_____

_____

_____

_____

_____

_____

_____

_____

_____

_____

_____

_____

_____

_____

Glossary of Terms

If your book has a number of difficult or rare words and concepts that will be confusing to your readers, you will need a *glossary*—an alphabetical list of these words at the back of the book explained in more detail—like a dictionary. A glossary is common in nonfiction books and is sometimes needed in fiction. (They are especially common in fantasy and sci-fi genres, where the author has created several unique terms in their world-building.)

If you have a word that is uncommon to your reader, it's good to explain it when you first introduce the term, so your reader doesn't have to look at the back of the book to find out what it means. But you also have the glossary at the back so that if you mention the term again, they can always look it up if they've forgotten what it means.

What terms do I need to include in the glossary?

_____

_____

_____

_____

_____

_____

Have I explained each term when I've introduced it for the first time in my book?   Yes ☐ No ☐

Do I have a glossary at the back of my book?   Yes ☐ No ☐

Index

An index helps your readers quickly find the information they are trying to find in your nonfiction book. It is an alphabetical list of subjects, names, places, and themes you are talking about in your book. It usually appears at the end of the book and gives the page numbers of where that information appears in the book.

Do you need an index at the back of your book? If you have a nonfiction book, it may be a good idea, but it's not a must-have. The benefits of having one are that it enhances your book's value and credibility, and some readers expect to find one at the back of the book.

I wouldn't recommend manually doing an index. It takes too much time and is prone to too many mistakes. You could hire a professional indexer, although this is often quite costly. It is much quicker and more reliable to simply create a list of entries (e.g., the words you want to index) and then give this list of entries to your layout designer. Your designer can create the index in InDesign at the click of a button, so in terms of their time and your cost, it is not prohibitive. Just ask them to include it in their quote.

Will I include an index in the back of my book?   Yes ☐ No ☐

Ads for Your Other Books

This is an excellent opportunity to promote your previously published books or your upcoming titles.

What other titles could you include at the back of your book?

_____

_____

_____

_____

_____

_____

Affiliate Links in Your Book

Do you regularly refer to products and services in your nonfiction book that you use and would recommend to others? Then it's a good idea to become an affiliate of that product or service and put your affiliate links throughout your book. In this way you earn a fee from anyone who decides to purchase that product/service using the affiliate link you supplied. It is at no extra cost to your reader, but it's an excellent way of earning an extra income from your book. Obviously, you will need to declare this at the front of the book in a disclaimer. You can use the affiliate disclosure clause included at the front of this book.

What products and services do you regularly recommend to others?

_____

_____

_____

_____

I have become an affiliate of the products I regularly
recommend so I earn a percentage of sales each time a
reader purchases a product from my affiliate link: Yes ☐ No ☐

Sponsored Ads at the Back of Your Book

This is also a great opportunity for you to get paid by complementary organizations with a similar target market by putting ads in the back of the book for their products and services. For example, if you have a gluten-free cookbook, you could approach organizations with gluten-free products you've used, which you want to recommend to your readers, and offer those organizations the opportunity to purchase a quarter-page, half-page, or full-page ad in the back of your book. What a brilliant way to recoup some of the costs of publishing your book!

What organizations could you approach to advertise their products and services in the back of your book?

_____

_____

_____

_____

Work with Me Page

If you have a nonfiction book, you may like to include a Work with Me page at the back of your book. This lets your readers know you are available for one-on-one mentoring, consultations, workshops, memberships, courses, programs, retreats, and presentations.

Remember your book can serve as a "business card on steroids" and allow people to get an in-depth knowledge into what it is you do or your message or story. It can lead to all sorts of opportunities, such as paid speaking and consulting if you plan to do those activities in the future. Make sure you add in your contact details so people can contact you by email, website, and social media.

MY WORK WITH ME PAGE

What would I like to offer my readers? Options include one-on-one mentoring, consulting, services, workshops, group coaching, programs, and speaking engagements. Specifically, what topics would I like to speak about?

_____

_____

_____

_____

_____

_____

_____

_____

_____

Contact Me Page

If you'd love to hear from your readers, let them know how they can connect with you.

EXAMPLE OF A CONTACT ME PAGE

Connect with Julie

info@iinspiremedia.com.au

iinspiremedia.com.au

facebook.com/JuliePostanceWritePublishandPromoteYourBook

facebook.com/The Heart-Centred Author (Writing, Self-Publishing and Marketing Books)

instagram.com/writepublishandpromoteyourbook

linkedin.com/in/JuliePostancePublishing

What will your Contact Me page say?

_____

_____

_____

_____

_____

_____

_____

_____

_____

Give Away Something for Free in Your Book to Build Your Email List

This is a really powerful marketing strategy that will have a significant impact on your future. Inside your book, in at least two places, you should mention that people can go to your website to get a free gift, 15-minute discovery call, video, e-course, free chapters of your new book, a quiz, a checklist, or a PDF that most of your readers will find valuable. Provide the URL in the hope that many of your readers will go to your website and input their email in return for the content you are giving away.

Once you have their emails, you can do several things: you can email them and ask them to leave a review on Amazon (improving social proof of your book and boosting sales), or you can email that content and updates that build more connection with your readers, tell them about your new books, promote other products and services, or promote other affiliate products. An email list is one of the most valuable things you can own.

What will you give away for free on your website?

_____

_____

_____

_____

_____

_____

_____

_____

Self-Publishing Success Story —Hugh Howey

Hugh Howey self-published his first few chapters of *Wool* as a US$0.99 novella on Kindle Direct Publishing in 2011. After he had quickly sold 1,000 copies, he redirected his energy toward writing more chapters. His next four e-book installments became bestsellers in several Amazon categories. In 2012, he released the full *Wool* e-book, which spent two weeks on the *New York Times* fiction bestseller list and was awarded the Kindle Book Review's 2012 Best Indie Book Award in the science fiction/fantasy category. Within a few months, Howey was selling 20,000–30,000 e-book copies a month, earning $150,000 a month. He became the first indie author to negotiate print-only rights with a mainstream publisher and retain his e-book rights (Klems 2014).

"The secret to being a writer is that you have to write. It's not enough to think about writing or to study literature or plan a future life as an author. You really have to lock yourself away, alone, and get to work."

—Augusten Burroughs, author of the bestselling memoir *Running with Scissors*

Taking a pause is exciting, invigorating, life changing and possible. Taking time out to see life from a different perspective or country can give us the energy and creativity to live life optimally.

4.

EDIT

"Kill your darlings, kill your darlings, even when it breaks your egocentric little scribbler's heart, kill your darlings."

—Stephen King, author of *On Writing: A Memoir of the Craft*

So, you've written the first draft of your manuscript—congratulations!

Now it's time to talk about editing.

This moves us away from the more creative, intuitive, expressive application of writing and toward a grammatical, logical, and structural approach to your manuscript. The amount of editing your book requires depends on how skilled you are as a writer and how much attention you paid to the language throughout the first draft. Fortunately, there are a number of ways to ensure you have dotted your i's and crossed all t's before you publish it.

The editing process is a critical part of the self-publishing journey, so use this chapter to determine what will be best for your book. Have you self-edited your work? Who will be your beta readers? Have you budgeted for a professional editor? And who will do the final proofread?

The answers to your questions will help you commit to a clear editing path. You'll also need to consider other factors, such as which version of English you'll decide to use (US, Canadian, UK, or Australian) and whether or not you'll require a style sheet, so you and your editor are on the same page. Read this chapter to understand what's involved throughout the editing process and adapt it to suit your book.

Step #1
Self-Edit Your Manuscript

Remember that your first draft is about getting down everything you wanted to say in your book. The next stage is about spending some time going through your manuscript, rewriting parts so it flows better, checking for missing words and typos, and making sure the grammar and punctuation is as good as you can get it before your beta readers and professional editor perfect it.

Ask yourself these questions as you go along:

- ❧ Should I move, add to, or cut this material?

- ❧ Is the style of writing appropriate for my target market?

- ❧ Are some of my sentences too long? Shorter sentences are easier to read—can I split this long sentence into two to three shorter sentences?

- ❧ Am I engaging my readers by speaking directly to them?

- ❧ Am I using jargon without explaining it?

- ❧ Could I put in more subheadings to make it clearer for my readers?

- ❧ Have I checked all facts, brand names, quotes, and references?

- ❧ Have I got all my front and back matter in my book, including Back Cover blurb, short and longer About the Author bios, Acknowledgements, Praise pages, and References?

The date I want to finish self-editing my manuscript is:

_____

_____

_____

I will devote _____ hours a day/week until I have finished self-editing my manuscript.

OR

I am committed to reading _____ pages a day/week until I have finished self-editing my manuscript.

Step #2
Get Feedback from 5–10 Beta Readers and Incorporate It into Your Book

Get feedback from 5–10 "beta readers" (or test readers), preferably in your target audience. They may also be colleagues, peers, or people whose opinions you value. These beta readers are a trusted group of people who will give you brutally honest, specific feedback about your title, subtitle, language, structure, style, voice, grammar, spelling, and anything else that needs improvement. This is key. Please don't approach family and friends who will just say how wonderful your book is! Your beta readers need to give you constructive feedback, which will later hopefully spare you the pain of receiving poor reviews on Amazon.

To ensure you get the most from your beta readers:

- Email them the whole book. Or if you don't want them to forget about it in their inbox, print off your book, on the front and back of each sheet of paper to minimize the amount of paper, and give it to them. Ask them to answer the following specific questions.

SPECIFIC BETA READER FEEDBACK QUESTIONS

1. Do you think my title is catchy? Does it tell the reader exactly what the book is about? Do you think there is a better title?

2. Do you think my subtitle tells you exactly what the book is about? Is there another subtitle you can think of?

3. Do you think my language is appropriate for my intended audience (insert your target market here)?

4. Do you think there is anything in my book that would offend or polarize readers?

5. What would you rate my book out of 10?

6. If you rated it less than a 10, how can I improve it to bring it up to a 10 out of 10?

7. Do you notice any issues with grammar, punctuation, or spelling? If so, please point them out to me.

❧ Ask them to answer your questions by a specific date, two weeks from the day you send it to them.

❧ Thank them, mention them in the Acknowledgments, and give them a free autographed copy of your book when it is published.

❧ As soon as you get their feedback, incorporate it into your book.

The deadline for my beta readers is:

_____

_____

_____

My deadline to incorporate all my beta readers' feedback into my book is:

_____

_____

Step #3
Get a Professional Editor for Your Book

Never compromise on a professional editor! You will risk scathing reviews on Amazon and elsewhere online, and if one of your first reviews is a one-star review criticizing your book for having typos, being badly edited, and "looking self-published," this will kill your online sales!

A professional editor usually does a *structural edit*—reviews the content of your writing (overall structure if it's nonfiction, and structure, characterization, pacing, plot, etc., if it's fiction) and a detailed *copyedit* (grammar, punctuation, and other technical errors). When you hire an editor, make sure they'll do both for you.

TIPS BEFORE YOU HIRE A PROFESSIONAL EDITOR

1. **Will your book be in US English, Canadian English, UK English, or Australian English?**

If your largest audience is in the US, it may be wise to use US English. Make sure you hire an editor who has experience following industry-recognized standards. If it's US English, *The Chicago Manual of Style* is considered the preferred style guide for book publishing. In Canada, the predominant style guide is *The Canadian Style: A Guide to Writing and Editing*. If it's British English, then you may use the *New Oxford Style Manual*. If you're using Australian English, you may use the *Style Manual for Authors, Editors and Printers*, 6th edition.

2. **If you need to, devise a short style sheet for your editor.**

A style sheet is a record of preferences for the purposes of consistency, professionalism, and ease of readability throughout the book. It allows the editor to keep track of decisions about spelling, punctuation, grammar, text layout, or in the case of fiction, characters' key features. If there is something you'd like the editor to do, then please make this clear before they start.

For example, in my book *Breaking the Sound Barriers*, I used both *Deaf* to refer to culturally Deaf or signing Deaf people and *deaf* to describe the condition of hearing loss as a general term. My first editor went through the book and incorrectly "corrected" all the upper-case *D*s to small *d*s. We could have saved so much time had I sent her a style sheet explaining the differences beforehand!

HOW DO I FIND A PROFESSIONAL EDITOR?

1. You can ask around for a recommendation, contact the professional association of editors in your city, or go to Upwork. com* and search for a specialist editor in your genre. You could also check the imprint page or acknowledgments for books you admire to see if the editor is listed. Then google their name. They may have a business website, a profile listed on Reedsy, or be available for hire through a site like Upwork*.

This is how to use Upwork*:

1. Go to Upwork.com* and register with your email address and a password. Here is a link: https://upwork.pxf.io/c/347458/1062918/13634

2. Post up a job specifying what you are looking for. For example: If you go searching for specialists in their field rather than posting the job yourself, you'll pay their normal rates, which are usually far higher (e.g., US$60 per hour). By posting what you're looking for and specifying your budget, you'll attract applicants specialized in this field who will either work for your specified budget or who will quote slightly lower or higher.

3. After a few days, you will have a number of candidates who have applied for your job. Read through their cover letters and résumés and have a look at their portfolio. Have they had experience in your genre, i.e., have they worked on books in the Christian genre that are now published? Delete all the applicants you think aren't suitable. I recommend choosing an applicant who has an above-90% job rating on Upwork*. Narrow down your search to one or two applicants.

> ## HIGHLY EXPERIENCED EDITOR TO ASSIST WITH GETTING A CHRISTIAN BOOK TO A MAINSTREAM PUBLISHABLE STANDARD.
>
> I need a highly experienced editor to assist with getting my Christian book about raising children to a publishable standard. This job is for one person. The book, which has approximately 15,000 words, needs help with the title and subtitle, the overall structure, rewording sentences, adding a bit more content to improve readability and flow, and a good edit to bring it to a publishable standard. Looking for someone who specializes in Christian books, who has previously edited Christian books, and someone who has worked on mainstream published books.
>
> Project Type: One-time project
> Skills: Editing, Writing
> Fixed Price
> Delivery by 4 December
> Budget US$375

4. Interview your two favorite applicants to see with whom you most resonate. Ask them specific questions about their experience. You can pay US$20–30 to have the two final applicants do a small one- to two-page sample for you. This will help to reveal if they are the right match for you. If you love their work, and you feel they will do a fantastic job for you, then hire them!

5. Break your job down into specific tasks and timeframes, e.g.,

    a. Edit first six chapters by [date by which you wish them to complete it].

    b. Edit last six chapters by [date by which you wish them to complete it].

6. Payment gets released only after you have seen and are satisfied with the job. If you aren't happy, follow up with the applicant or with Upwork*, and if you aren't able to resolve this matter, you can cancel the job.

The name of my Upwork* editor is:

_____

_____

_____

The breakdown of my tasks.

First _____ chapters by _____ (date).

Next _____ chapters by _____ date).

You have paid for the skills of your editor, so make sure you incorporate most of their recommendations. They are the expert, but don't be afraid to ask questions. If you're interested in knowing why a specific edit was made or would like to know more about a particular grammar or style rule, your editor should be able to explain it to you, provide a resource where you can learn more, or otherwise satisfy your question and help you become a better writer overall.

My deadline to incorporate my editor's feedback into my book is:

_____

TEST YOUR TITLE

You've tested your title and subtitle on your beta readers and your editor, but you can go one step further and test it on social media, Pickfu.com, or even do a Google Ads campaign!

You can do this for free with your friends on Facebook or Instagram. Ask them: "Which title do you like for my book about veganism: *The Book of Veganism* or *Vegan for Life*?"

You can also do a test of two or three titles on Pickfu.com with 50 respondents in the US starting at US$50. Here is the link: pickfu. com/industries/publishing

The most sophisticated way of testing a book title was done by Tim Ferriss, author of *The 4-Hour Work Week: Escape 9-5, Live Anywhere and Join the New Rich.*

He brainstormed six titles for his book including *The 4-Hour Work Week*, *Millionaire Chameleon*, and *Broadband and White Sand*, and created a Google Ads campaign for each one. He used keywords related to the content of the book (retirement, world travel, learning languages, etc.) so that when those keywords formed part of someone's search on Google, his title and ad text would come up. After one week and for less than $200, he was able to determine that *The 4-Hour Work Week* was the title that was the most clicked on, and this became the title of his book. Despite being a first-time author, Tim Ferriss's book went straight to the top of the *New York Times* Bestseller list because of his winning title (Ferris 2007).

Step #4
It's Time to Proofread Your Book!

PROOFREADING

Proofreading is checking for typos. It's best to pay your editor to proofread the text one more time after you've incorporated all their changes. Or hire a separate proofreader to do this. They won't have read the text before and therefore won't be as close to it as your original editor.

You also need to have a good read through of your own book before it goes to the typesetter. Then you can get the proofreader to proofread the typeset version again before it goes to print. It is important that you also proofread the book a few times before it goes to print. Even ask your friends to read it. Having multiple eyes on your book will ensure that most typos get picked up before the release of the final product.

There is nothing worse than finding typos in your published book once you have printed copies! Luckily, you can order a sample copy of your book before you make it live or before you order large quantities. Make sure you read it one more time and give any changes to the typesetter. The author always has the ultimate responsibility of ensuring their own book is typo-free.

The name of my proofreader is:

_____

My proofreader will proofread the Word version by:

_____

The proofreader will proofread the typeset version by:

_____

I proofread my own book before it went to the typesetter: Yes ☐ No ☐

I read my sample book before I made it live or ordered a large quantity: Yes ☐ No ☐

AVOID BEING SUED

Before you publish your book, get a lawyer to look over potentially libelous or defamatory paragraphs. You may get sued because you are the publisher, even if you simply quoted the words in your book!

Libel is defined as a false statement of fact "of and concerning" a person, which damages their reputation. Changing names is not enough if a person can prove that their reputation has suffered as a result of the memoir you wrote.

Self-Publishing Success Story —William Paul Young

William Paul Young originally wrote the book *The Shack* for his six children to disclose his own painful journey to "light, love and transformation." He produced 15 copies, which he gave to family and friends for Christmas. Two of his friends, Jacobson and Cummings, loved it so much, they helped him rewrite it and shipped it off to 24 publishers, all of whom flatly rejected it. They decided to self-publish and sold it from their website in 2007. It gained huge momentum, taking four months to sell 11,000 copies. They ordered 22,000 more copies, which sold out in two months. A third print run of 33,000 copies sold out in a month. By 2008, it had reached #1 on the *New York Times* Bestseller list. In 2008, Hachette took over distribution. By 2017, they had sold more than 22 million copies. The book was adapted for a movie in 2017, featuring Sam Worthington, which achieved $96.9 million at the box office (Hughes 2011).

5.

COVER

"There are three responses to a piece of design—yes, no, and WOW! Wow is the one to aim for."

—Milton Glaser, author of *The Design of Dissent*

Whether you like it or not, your book will be judged by its cover. I have devoted an entire chapter to discussing cover design, as it is a critical part of your book. You've come this far on the journey—now is not the time to fall short on quality, professionalism, and attention to detail.

A book cover is the *first impression*. It is the initial point of contact your book will have with potential buyers when they browse a bookstore or surf Amazon. There is power inherent in this moment! A book buyer's decision is heavily influenced by the cover—you already know this to be true. It is also a major feature that distributors or bookstore owners look at before considering whether to take on your book. If your cover appears homemade, unprofessional, or aesthetically dull, they will move on to the next—as simple as that.

We want your front cover to elicit an emotional gut response that compels a potential buyer to flip it over and read the back cover or click on the link to the book's description. If your front and back covers don't hook them in, you've lost the sale. Readers who surf and skim the online book market spend mere seconds eyeing the covers, so you need to entice and attract them rapidly. On average, a person spends *five to eight* seconds on a cover that they find interesting, as opposed to spending only *one to three* seconds on an unappealing cover.

Look at it like this: your front and back cover are the prime real estate of your book. Every element—the title, subtitle, image, color, and back cover blurb—is of utmost importance. The sum of these parts and how they are presented can make or break the success of your book. If your book cover says boring, outdated, or poor quality in any way, you are literally decreasing your sales.

A fantastic book cover design is something to get excited about. Now is the time to get creative and seek the skills of a professional cover designer. There are cover must-haves, there is market research to be done, and there are specific details each cover requires. And besides, you want to be able to hold your book and be proud of every inch of its creation. The choices you make now will impact that moment—how does the dream look, feel, vibe? Let's create *that*.

Goal: To finish my cover design. The date I want to achieve this is:

_____

YOUR COVER MUST-HAVES

- One strong, clear graphic (not busy and never a collage!).

- An emotional tug.

- A catchy title that can be read from several feet away on a bookstand and is easy to read as a small JPEG image when viewed on a phone.

- Author name in smaller font than the title, unless you are well known.

- Your cover has been tested on your target readers and voted as the favorite (see pages 174–175).

RESEARCH YOUR COVER

Before you do anything else, do some market research in your chosen niche. Go to Amazon, type in the subject of your chosen niche, and then have a look at the particular covers that come up. (For example, if you're putting together a cookbook built around the Paleo diet, search Paleo diet cookbooks.) What are the bestselling books in your niche? If they are bestselling, their covers are obviously resonating with their target market. Save the book covers you like into a folder on your computer as part of your research. Pick out the elements you prefer and discard the elements you don't like.

Most book covers suit their genre well. For example:

- **Business** or **self-help** books often display a picture of the author as the expert surrounded by a blocky title font.

- **Literary novels** often feature a whimsical, decorated, or cursive-style title font with soft shades of color and possibly a contemplative picture or imagery.

- **Romance novel** covers usually have a man or woman (or both), locked in a close embrace or gazing passionately at each other.

- **Thrillers or action/adventure** covers display the author's name and title in big, bold lettering, superimposed on a graphical representation of a main story element.

Based on your research, what did you notice as common design elements of your genre?

_____

_____

_____

What do you want your cover to look like?

_____

_____

_____

WHERE CAN I GET MY BOOK COVER DESIGNED?

These days, I go to two websites to have my own book covers and those of my clients and students designed.

ON A BUDGET? USE GETCOVERS.COM

On Getcovers.com, you can get an eye-catching, print-ready and e-book cover design for between US$20–$35. With unlimited free revisions, a 100% money-back guarantee, licensed images and fonts, four- to five-day delivery time, and marketing materials for social media etc., this is a fantastic option for the indie author.

The covers that emerge from Getcovers are striking and professional, and their team (who are based in Ukraine) are polite and eager to bring your book's essence to life. The only downside is you only get one cover as opposed to up to 250 designs that you get from 99designs* (see below). So you might need to purchase a few covers or return to the designer several times before you get a cover that truly captures your vision.

THE BEST OPTION HANDS DOWN FOR A PROFESSIONAL COVER DESIGN —99DESIGNS.COM*

Hands down, the best website to get your book cover designed is 99designs.com*. Here is the link: https://99designs.qvig.net/c/347458/177079/3172. This website currently has more than 1 million designers located all over the world who bid on the work posted there. Many are award-winning designers providing exceptional designs for you, and you will only have to pay for the design you like! If you don't like any of the designs, you don't have to pay.

How it works is you post up a simple description of how you'd like your book cover to look. You choose your price point—from US$299 up to US$1,499. The more you offer to pay, the more designers will submit designs to you.

I recommend choosing the US$299 option, as in my experience with clients and students, they tend to get between 50–250 designs, which is more than enough to choose from. If you get fewer designs than this, please call 99designs.com*, and they will support you in getting more designs for your book cover contest.

Once you have posted your design brief (see example on page 170), your design contest will be listed on the website, and designers from all over the world will submit book cover designs onto the website. Over the course of four days, designs will be submitted, and your job will be to provide feedback to the designers in the form of eliminating the designs you don't like, giving the remaining designs star ratings out of five, and commenting on their designs, i.e., *Please increase the font*, or *Please move the photo to the left*, etc.

You then have four days to pick six designers to work with in the final round. Over the following three days, you will help them revise the final designs. You then have up to two weeks to choose your winning design. You will both sign an electronic copyright agreement to transfer full copyright to you, and the winning designer will be paid. The winning designer needs to come up with all the book files you need to publish your book on the different publishing platforms.

Tip: You don't have to have all the necessary cover elements to start your cover. You can provide your back cover blurb, logo, barcode, etc. as you go and even after you have chosen your winning designer. The main objective is just to *start*, and you will find you'll gather momentum once you start working with the designers.

If you do not wish to use AI or stock images, then please specify this in your brief.

To set up a cover design on 99designs* go to https://99designs.qvig.net/c/347458/177079/3172.

AN EXAMPLE OF A BRIEF ON 99DESIGNS.COM*

I would like you to design a beautiful book cover (front, back, and spine) for my nonfiction book that explores how nature sustains human health and well-being.

The title of this book is *Nature, Our Medicine*, and the subtitle is *How the Natural World Sustains Us*. Author name: Dr. Dimity Williams. Target audience is primarily women aged 30 and above who are interested in nature and the environment. The printed book dimensions will be 6x9 inches.

Please note that you will be expected to create the files for IngramSpark (in paperback and hardback) and Kindle Direct Publishing (paperback).

I have attached screenshots of images and fonts as design inspiration, the publishing logo, back cover blurb, and barcode. I look forward to seeing your creativity!

Dimity Williams received a total of 68 designs and narrowed it down to a final eight. These were then tweaked to try different combinations of fonts and colors. Dimity did a poll with friends and others in the Authentic Author program and two clear favorites were picked. Dimity says, "It was difficult to choose from the final couple, which were stunning! I landed on the current cover because the ECG symbol is synonymous with medicine, and the butterflies and leaves bring nature into it—just as the title says 'nature is medicine.'"

Figure 6. Front and back cover of *Nature, Our Medicine* by Dr. Dimity Williams. Reproduced with kind permission from Dimity Williams and Currawong Books. *Nature, Our Medicine*, 2023, first published by Currawong Books.

"Aspiring authors, get this through your head. Cover art serves one purpose, and one purpose only, to get potential customers interested long enough to pick up the book to read the back cover blurb. In the internet age that means the thumbnail image needs to be interesting enough to click on. That's what covers are for."

—Larry Correia, American fantasy novelist of Monster Hunter and Grimnoir Chronicles series.

What You Will Need for Your Cover

- ❧ **Title**

- ❧ **Subtitle**

- ❧ **Author name or names**

- ❧ **A strong emotive image** that grabs the attention of your target market. Unless you request your own image be used, if you are using 99designs.com* or Getcovers.com, they will provide images for you, usually from a royalty-free website such as iStockPhoto.com. Always ask for the link to the source of their image so you can check to make sure it's royalty free and so you can purchase your own license for this image. Even if the photo is free, you will need to sign up for your own account and download it so that it is licensed under your name. Make sure you download the extra-large image so you can use the large image on promotional banners, etc. If you are using an image that you have sourced, please ensure that you have correctly purchased and licensed the image or obtained permission to use it or that it's one from the public domain; otherwise, you may leave yourself open to copyright infringement.

- ❧ **Your compelling back cover blurb**

- ❧ **Your author bio and pic.** You only need this for a nonfiction book. See page 70.

- ❧ **Two to three testimonials.** You can ask for these from your beta readers who read your book in the editing process, or you can send out a chapter or your whole book to two or three individuals and request a testimonial before your book is published. If you have a lot of testimonials, use your best ones. This will give your book far more credibility.

- ❧ **Your barcode** (with your ISBN above it). The barcode identifies the ISBN, which identifies your book details. If you don't put a barcode on the back of your book, your book will immediately look self-published and won't be taken seriously by bookstores. You can either buy this when you purchase your ISBNs at Bowker.com or go to https://bookow.com/resources.php and purchase one by donation. Your paperback and hardback versions need a barcode but not your e-books.

❧ **Your publishing logo.** You can get this designed at Fiverr.com*. Here is a link: https://fvrr.co/2SxlAAV. Give them the publishing name that you registered and request a 300dpi JPEG image and a transparent PNG image that will go on the bottom lefthand side of the back cover as well as the bottom of the spine.

❧ **Your website URL.** This is your domain name that you purchased from Godaddy.com.

YOUR COVER CHECKLIST

My title is:

_____

My subtitle is:

_____

My author name or names:

_____

My strong emotive image is:

_____

My compelling back cover blurb has been edited by my professional editor: Yes ☐   No ☐

I have a professional author photo: Yes ☐   No ☐

I have two or three of my best testimonials for my back cover: Yes ☐ No ☐

I have separate barcodes that have the corresponding ISBNs for my paperback and hardback versions of my book: Yes ☐ No ☐

I have my publishing logo from Fiverr.com* as a 300dpi JPEG and PNG: Yes ☐ No ☐

I have purchased my domain name for my website from Godaddy.com: Yes ☐ No ☐

TEST YOUR COVER ON YOUR TARGET READERS

Have you tested your cover on your target readers? This is probably the most important step, as they will be the buyers of your book! So many times, I have witnessed my students test their covers on others in my programs only to be told "What does the title mean?" or "What does the subtitle mean?" or "Sorry, your cover tells me nothing about what your book is about," or "Your cover looks more like a romance novel, not a science fiction novel."

It is not enough for your family to say that they love your book cover. They aren't your target readers. When I had my book cover for my book *Breaking the Sound Barriers* designed, my designer gave me two samples: one with a blue background and one with an orange background. I was convinced that the orange one was perfect. However, when I tested it on my target audience, every one of them said they loved the blue but not the orange one! My opinion in this instance was irrelevant. Families of deaf children were the target readers of this book, and they preferred the blue, so needless to say, the cover ended up being blue. You need to take your readers' preferences into account.

I have tested my covers on members of my target market:　　　　Yes ☐　No ☐

POLL YOUR TARGET AUDIENCE ABOUT YOUR COVER

One of the best things about 99designs.com* is having a multitude of great designs from which to choose. But with so many options, it can sometimes be hard to decide which design you like best!

If you'd like help deciding which design to choose, why not create a poll using the polling tool? With a poll, you can get your friends, colleagues, and social network to vote on up to eight designs they like in order of preference and help you decide.

I did a poll on 99designs.com* to choose my winning cover:　　　　Yes ☐　No ☐

INDECISIVE ABOUT YOUR FINAL TWO COVERS?

Use Pickfu.com. If you are having issues deciding which two covers to use, or which title to use, you can get unbiased feedback from 50 US respondents for US$50 within an hour!

I used Pickfu.com to choose my winning cover:　　　　Yes ☐　No ☐

WHERE CAN I BUY IMAGES FOR MY COVER?

If you wish to use your book to promote your business, then you may decide to use a photo of yourself on the front cover. Hiring a professional photographer for your images is recommended. Do you have a friend who is a professional photographer? Ask them to take your photos. Otherwise ask for a recommendation or search for a photographer on Google, Instagram or Facebook.

If you are working with 99designs.com* or Fiverr.com*, they will source an image for you unless you advise them to use one you have chosen on the cover. You can upload this photo when you do your brief on 99designs.com*.

You can find a royalty-free image for your cover at these websites:

❧ iStockPhoto.com

❧ Dreamstime.com

❧ Flickr.com

❧ Shutterstock.com

❧ Depositphotos.com

❧ Unsplash.com

Most photos come under a standard license that permits you to sell up to 500,000 copies of your book. If you sell more than that, you'll need to purchase your image under an extended license.

Rather than use a photograph, you may choose to hire an artist to provide an illustration for your book cover. You can buy illustrated photos online, find illustrations or graphics that are licensed for commercial use, or hire an artist to create custom work for you. In any case, be sure your illustrations are a minimum of 300 dpi JPEG files so they are high-resolution enough to print. Anything less than that will look messy and unprofessional.

If the image I want to use is copyrighted, I've requested permission from the copyright holder:	Yes ☐ No ☐
I have purchased the high-resolution image (minimum 300 dpi JGEG) and have a license to use it:	Yes ☐ No ☐

A Note on Spine Width

Most cover designers will ask you for the spine width measurement, but you won't know the spine width until your book has been typeset to be published. The spine width for a printed book is determined by the number of typeset pages, the thickness of text paper stock, and the thickness of the cover. Once your book has been laid out for print, ask your book formatter/graphic designer for the spine width, and give it to your cover designer to finalize.

#GENIUS TIP—CHILDREN'S BOOKS!

If you're writing a children's book (or another book for which you plan to include a lot of artwork or illustrations), you'll need to hire the same artist to create both the cover art and interior artwork for that book and others in the series. This will ensure an overall consistent appearance and a higher quality product.

So when choosing a cover designer for your children's book, please make sure that the creator of the cover used original illustrations on the cover and not stock or AI images (unless you want an AI-illustrated book). When selecting a cover, ask the designer if the work is original and whether they would be willing to illustrate your entire children's book. It's even better if they can do the cover, full illustrations, and layout of the book. Negotiate this with them prior to awarding them the winning cover design. Then you can set up a separate 99designs.com* job for the rest of the illustrations and layout. If they can only do the illustrations, that's fine, too, but you'll have to find a formatter to do the layout of your book.

Where else can I find an illustrator to do my children's book? You can search Google, Instagram, Fiverr.com* or Facebook groups such as *Children's Book Authors and Illustrators: Publishing, Marketing and Selling* or find a local recommendation.

Self-Publishing Success Story—Melissa Leong

Melissa Leong is a well-known business journalist. She decided to write her YA vampire novel, *What Kills Me*, under the pen name Wynne Channing and sent it to agents, as she wanted a traditional publishing deal. Not one of them was interested, which she wrote in a *National Post* article "was like death by 1,000 paper cuts." Her friends convinced her to self-publish.

She set the price at US$2.99 on Amazon but hardly sold any copies, so she reduced the price to US$0.99 to attract more readers and became a bestseller in the Occult and Action & Adventure categories. *What Kills Me* and *I Am Forever* have now sold more than 70,000 copies (Leong 2012).

"Don't quit. Never give up trying to build the world you can see, even if others can't see it. Listen to your drum and your drum only. It's the one that makes the sweetest sound."

—Simon Sinek, author of *Start with Why: How Great Leaders Inspire Everyone to Take Action*

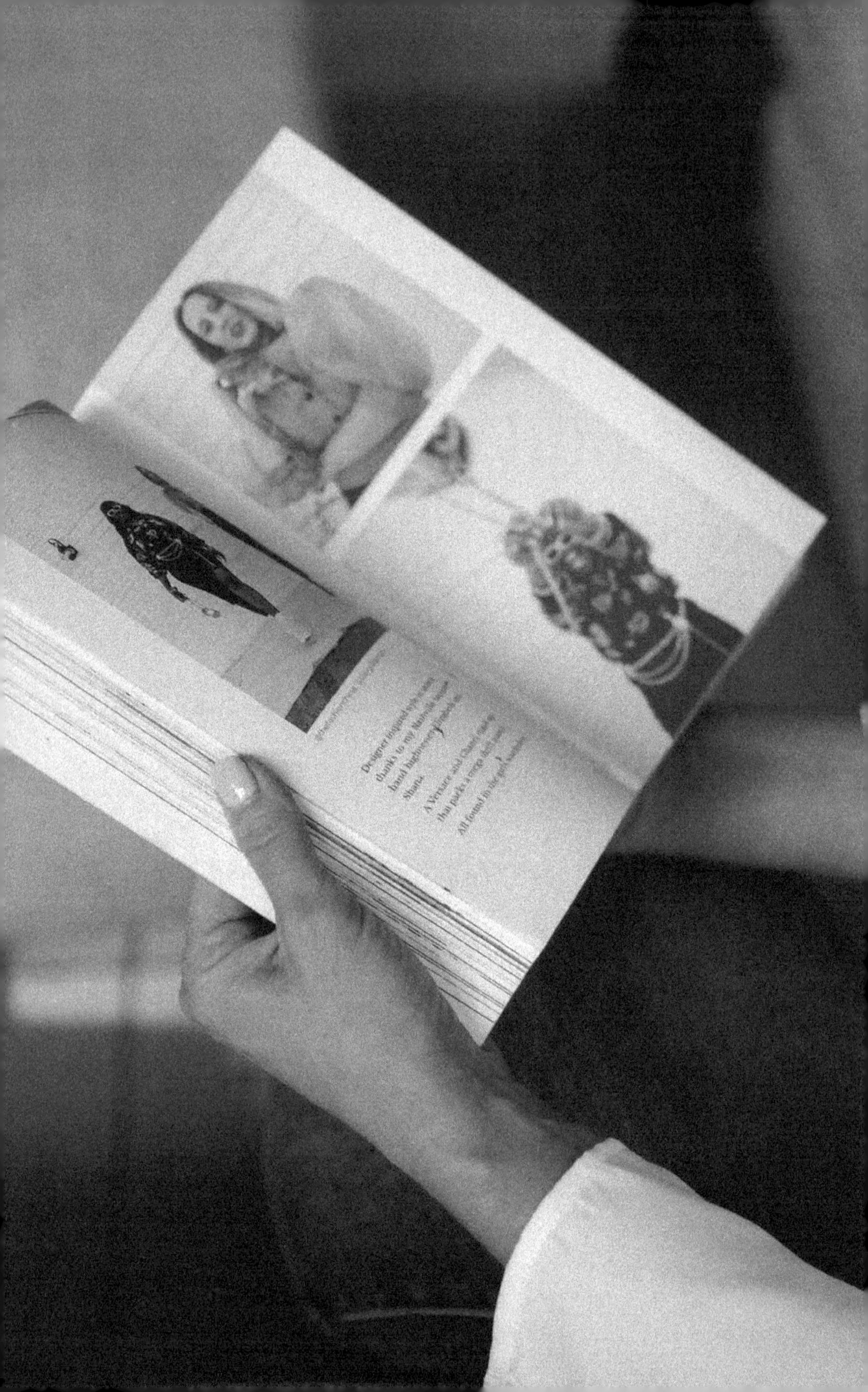

6.

LAYOUT

"I strive for two things in design: simplicity and clarity. Great design is born of those two things."

—Lindon Leader, American graphic designer and recipient of more than 30 prestigious design awards worldwide

You've put a lot of time and effort into writing your book, and you want your book's interior to reflect that. Typesetting or book formatting is the process of laying out your text and images beautifully to prepare it to print a paperback or hardback book that provides an enjoyable reading experience. A graphic designer or a book typesetter or formatter can typeset your book beautifully in readiness for publication. Below I've provided a few options when it comes to finding the right designer who can help realize your vision of a stunning book interior. I have also outlined a thorough overview of what's required to complete your layout with style and sophistication. By the end of this process, you'll have reached a turning point—you are so very close to the publishing finishing line! So be sure to fill out the checklist at the end of this chapter in readiness for the finale.

How Do You Find the Perfect Graphic Designer for Your Book?

Here are some ideas:

1. Get a recommendation from someone who has worked with a fabulous book designer.

2. Go to a bookstore or a library and find some book layouts that you love. Look at the imprint page for the name of the designer and contact them for a quote.

3. Set up a design contest on 99designs.com˙. Here is the link: https://99designs.qvig.net/c/347458/177079/3172

4. Search Google for a book designer in your area.

5. Set up a brief on Upwork.com˙. Here is the link: https://upwork.pxf.io/c/347458/1062918/13634

6. Try out some designers on Fiverr.com˙. Here is a link: https://fvrr.co/2SxlAAV

Make sure you only select a graphic designer/formatter/typesetter who uses Adobe InDesign to create your book. InDesign is a powerful design software that will ensure you get the high-quality interior that your book deserves. Make sure you let them know that you'd like the packaged InDesign files at the end of the project; having the files in your possession means you can have any other graphic designer create the required files to publish your paperback and hardback on IngramSpark and your paperback and e-book on Kindle Direct Publishing. It also means that any other designer can make changes to your files in the future, and you won't have to return to the particular designer who did the initial work. After all, you have paid for the files, and you now own them, so you should have them in a folder on your computer.

WHAT TO DO ONCE YOU'VE FOUND YOUR DESIGNER

These are your next steps:

1. Go to a bookstore or a library. Have a look at popular books in your genre and measure their dimensions. Find the size of a book you like and make a note of its measurement in inches. Or go to Amazon.com and compare the size of several bestsellers in your genre. You can find the printed book dimensions when you scroll down to the Product Details section of the paperback or hardback version. Certain sizes are standard in certain genres (see *Most Popular Book Sizes* on page 189).

2. Find the closest standard industry book size on the publishing platforms you will use, i.e., IngramSpark and Kindle Direct Publishing. The standard book sizes for both platforms are listed on page 188 and 189. Standard book sizes are offered in inches (width x height). It will be easier for your formatter to choose the same book size for both platforms. If you are going to do a hardback version, make sure the size you've chosen can

be done in paperback and hardback on IngramSpark as well as paperback on KDP, so the book designer keeps the same size for all three formats. And if you choose a children's book or cookbook, make sure you go for one of the sizes available for an IngramSpark *premium color* book.

3. By looking through other books, you can find the layout, spacing, and font you like. When you do, take photos of them, and send them to your typesetter/graphic designer. Ask them to do something similar with your book. Alternatively, you can leave it up to their own creative expertise.

4. Don't forget your book must have a minimum of 24 pages, and the final page count must be a multiple of four.

5. Send your finished Word document book template plus all your images as separate JPEG files (preferably in 300dpi) to your typesetter/graphic designer. Make it clear on your document where the images are supposed to appear. Caption all the graphics and credit them to the photographers or illustrators.

6. Ensure you have permission to use the stories and photos from your contributors—you'll want to avoid legal claims down the track. Download the Story and Images Permission Form from www.iinspiremedia.com.au.

7. When you get the book layout back, it will be in a PDF file. Review the PDF and send any changes you would like made to the typesetter. It's more efficient and easier for the designer to do the edits directly onto the PDF file itself, so have your typesetter implement any changes.

8. Once your designer sends back the second/final PDF file with your changes implemented, send the final PDF file (called a "proof") to a professional proofreader or your editor for one last proofread before it goes to print.

9. Proofread the book yourself several times before it goes to print.

Check to see that your page numbers are correct, that your contents page matches up to the chapter titles, that your imprint page is perfect, that your images are all captioned, and that there are no typos.

10. Your cover designer and/or typesetter needs to supply you with the files I have listed below. *I recommend doing the IngramSpark paperback version first and ordering a sample from IngramSpark.* Once you see the printed sample, you'll no doubt have changes, which you can then give a list of those changes to the typesetter/cover designer, who can then implement those changes across all versions (paperback, hardback, and e-book), saving on cost.

IngramSpark Standard Book Sizes

PAPERBACK BOOKS

Trade paperback books available with perfect binding are the most popular. Perfect binding is a process commonly used by printers and bookmakers where groups of pages are bound together using adhesive to create a clean, crisp, and professionally printed product. To get a perfect bound paperback book, you'll need a minimum of 24 pages, although to have a spine on your book, you'll need a minimum of 48 pages. See the table on page 188 for available sizes, or for the complete list go to: https://www.ingramspark.com/hubfs/downloads/trim-sizes.pdf

HARDCOVER BOOKS

Hardcover books are available in case laminate, cloth, or jacketed. Case laminate means the cover pages are glued to hard coverings at the ends. See the table on page 188 for available sizes, or for the complete list go to: https://www.ingramspark.com/hubfs/downloads/trim-sizes.pdf

STANDARD COLOR BOOKS

Standard color offers a more economical option for publishers who don't require the high quality of premium color. See the table on page 188 for available sizes, or for the complete list go to: https://www.ingramspark.com/hubfs/downloads/trim-sizes.pdf

PREMIUM COLOR BOOKS
AND ULTRA-PREMIUM COLOR BOOKS

Premium color is perfect for children's books, cookbooks, or coffee table books that are rich in graphics. Ultra-premium color is the best color quality, ideal for photography books, coffee table books, and high-quality children's books and gives your book a glossier look.

#GENIUS TIP!

Only choose a color interior for your book if it's absolutely necessary.

It's important to note having a color book is substantially more expensive than black and white. For example, on IngramSpark, a 6"x9", 200-page, black-and-white paperback book costs US$4.08 to print (not including shipping, etc.).

The same book in standard color 50 costs US$6.78; in standard color 70, US$8.40; in premium color, US$15.00; and in ultra-premium color, US$17.50.

You can check this yourself here: https://myaccount.ingramspark.com/Portal/Tools/ShippingCalculator

If you have a children's book or a book rich in graphics, then your customers will expect it to be in premium color. Otherwise consider whether you can do your book in black and white—your book royalties will be better for it!

INGRAM SPARK SIZES

For the complete list go to:
https://www.ingramspark.com/hubfs/
downloads/trim-sizes.pdf

inches	mm	binding*	B&W				COLOUR		PREMIUM
			Groundwood	Creme	50 lb White	70 lb White	50 lb White	70 lb White	70 lb White
4 × 6	152 × 102	PB	✓	✓	✓	✓	✓	✓	✓
4 × 7	178 × 102	PB		✓	✓	✓	✓	✓	✓
4.25 × 7	178 × 108	PB		✓	✓	✓	✓	✓	✓
4.37 × 7	178 × 111	PB	✓		✓	✓	✓	✓	
4.72 × 7.48	190 × 120	PB		✓	✓	✓	✓	✓	
5 × 7	178 × 127	PB	✓	✓	✓	✓	✓	✓	
5 × 8	203 × 127	PB, CL	✓	✓	✓	✓	✓	✓	✓
		DC, JC			✓	✓	✓	✓	✓
5.06 × 7.81	198 × 129	PB	✓	✓	✓	✓	✓	✓	
5.25 × 8	203 × 133	PB	✓	✓	✓	✓	✓	✓	
5.5 × 7.5	191 × 140	PB	✓		✓	✓	✓	✓	
5.5 × 8.25	210 × 140	PB	✓	✓	✓	✓	✓	✓	✓
5.5 × 8.38	213 × 140	PB	✓	✓					
5.5 × 8.5	216 × 140	PB, CL, DC, JC	✓	✓	✓	✓	✓	✓	✓
5.83 × 8.27	210 × 148	PB, CL	✓	✓	✓	✓	✓	✓	
6 × 9	229 × 152	PB, CL, DC, JC	✓	✓	✓	✓	✓	✓	✓
6.14 × 9.21	234 × 156	PB, CL, DC, JC	✓	✓	✓	✓	✓	✓	
6.5 × 6.5	165 × 165	PB			✓	✓	✓	✓	✓
6.625 × 10.25	260 × 168	PB			✓	✓	✓	✓	✓
6.69 × 9.61	244 × 170	PB, CL			✓	✓	✓	✓	✓
7 × 10	254 × 178	PB, CL			✓	✓	✓	✓	✓
7.44 × 9.69	246 × 189	PB			✓	✓	✓	✓	
7.50 × 9.25	235 × 191	PB, CL			✓	✓	✓	✓	✓
8 × 8	203 × 203	PB, CL			✓	✓	✓	✓	✓
8 × 10	254 × 203	PB, CL			✓	✓	✓	✓	✓
8 × 10.88	276 × 203	PB, CL			✓	✓	✓	✓	✓
8.25 × 10.75	273 × 210	PB, CL			✓	✓	✓	✓	✓
8.25 × 11	280 × 210	PB			✓	✓	✓	✓	✓
8.268 × 11.693	297 × 210	PB			✓	✓	✓	✓	
8.5 × 8.5	216 × 216	PB, CL			✓	✓	✓	✓	✓
8.5 × 9	229 × 216	PB			✓	✓	✓	✓	✓
8.5 × 11	280 × 216	PB, CL			✓	✓	✓	✓	✓
11 × 8.5	216 × 280	PB, CL			✓	✓	✓	✓	✓

*Paperback option: PB = Perfectbound
*Hardcover options: CL = Case Laminate, DC = Digital Cloth Cover (Blue/Gray), JC = Jacketed Cover

KDP SIZES

For the complete list go to: https://kdp.amazon.com/en_US/help/topic/G201834180

inches	mm	binding*	B&W Creme	B&W White	COLOUR White	PREMIUM White
5 × 8	203 × 127	PB	✓	✓	✓	✓
5.06 × 7.81	198 × 129	PB	✓	✓	✓	✓
5.25 × 8	203 × 133	PB	✓	✓	✓	✓
5.5 × 8.5	210 × 140	PB	✓	✓	✓	✓
		CL	✓	✓		✓
6 × 9	229 × 152	PB	✓	✓	✓	✓
		CL	✓	✓		✓
6.14 × 9.21	234 × 156	PB	✓	✓	✓	✓
		CL	✓	✓		✓
6.69 × 9.61	244 × 170	PB	✓	✓	✓	✓
7 × 10	254 × 178	PB	✓	✓	✓	✓
		CL	✓	✓		✓
7.44 × 9.69	246 × 189	PB	✓	✓	✓	✓
7.50 × 9.25	235 × 191	PB	✓	✓	✓	✓
8 × 10	254 × 203	PB	✓	✓	✓	✓
8.25 × 6	210 × 152	PB	✓	✓	✓	✓
8.25 × 8.25	210 × 210	PB	✓	✓	✓	✓
8.268 × 11.693	297 × 210	PB	✓	✓	✓	✓
8.5 × 8.5	216 × 216	PB	✓	✓	✓	✓
8.5 × 11	280 × 216	PB	✓	✓	✓	✓
8.25 × 11	210 × 279	CL	✓	✓		✓

*Paperback option: PB = Perfectbound. Hardcover option: CL = Case Laminate.

MOST POPULAR SIZES

inches	mm	Popular for
5 × 8	203 × 127	General Fiction, Novella, Inspirational/Spiritual, Middle-Grade Fiction
5.25 × 8	203 × 133	General Fiction, Thrillers/Mysteries, General Self-Help, Memoir, Business
5.5 × 8.5	210 × 140	General Fiction, General Nonfiction, YA Dystopian, Fantasy, and Sci-Fi, Memoir, Business
6 × 9	229 × 152	General Fiction, General Nonfiction, Reference, Textbooks
7 × 10	254 × 178	General Nonfiction, Reference, Textbooks
8 × 10	254 × 203	Picture Books
8.5 × 11	280 × 216	Textbooks
8.5 × 8.5	216 × 216	Picture Books

Kindle Direct Publishing Standard Book Sizes

PAPERBACK BOOKS

See the table on page 189 for available sizes, or for the complete list go to https://kdp.amazon.com/en_US/help/topic/G201834180.

HARDBACK BOOKS

Hardcover books are printed as case laminate. This means your hardcover book will not have a dust jacket and the artwork is printed directly on the cover. The minimum page count is 75 pages. There are currently very limited available sizes (see page 192), so chances are you'll be publishing your hardback through IngramSpark, as they have a greater number of size options. See the table on 189 for available sizes, or for the complete list go to https://kdp.amazon.com/en_US/help/topic/G201834180

#GENIUS TIP!

Would you like your title and author name to show on the spine of your book?

Being able to see the title and author name on the spine of your book is important so your book can be seen and found on the store, library, or home bookshelf.

If you'd like your book to have spine text, you need to make your book a minimum of 79 typeset pages for Kindle Direct Publishing, a minimum of 48 typeset pages for an IngramSpark paperback, and a minimum of 18 typeset pages for an IngramSpark hardback.

Files You Will Need for Your Printed Book

1.   IngramSpark Paperback Cover

Front cover, back cover, and spine in PDF format for IngramSpark. Your cover designer will need to follow the IngramSpark cover submission guidelines. Here is the most up-to-date link to the IngramSpark submission guidelines: chrome-extension:// efaidnbmnnnibpcajpcglclefindmkaj/https://www.ingramspark. com/hubfs/downloads/file-creation-guide.pdf

2.   IngramSpark Paperback Interior

Interior PDF for IngramSpark. Your formatter will need to follow the IngramSpark submission guidelines.

3.   IngramSpark Hardback Cover

This will be either case laminate with or without a dust jacket, or digital cloth with or without a dust jacket. Digital cloth is a clothlike look (available with or without dust jacket). It has a textured feel and is available for hardcover books printed in the US and UK only. Your cover designer will need to follow the IngramSpark hardback cover submission guidelines.

4.   IngramSpark Hardback Interior

Your layout designer can use the same interior file as the paperback interior.

5.   Kindle Direct Publishing (KDP) Paperback Cover

Front cover, back cover, and spine PDF for Kindle Direct Publishing. Your cover designer will need to follow the Kindle Direct Publishing cover submission guidelines. Here is the most up-to-date link to the KDP submission guidelines: https://kdp.amazon.com/en_US/help/ topic/G201857950

6. Kindle Direct Publishing (KDP) Paperback Interior

Interior PDF for Kindle Direct Publishing. Your formatter will need to follow the KDP interior submission guidelines.

7. Kindle Direct Publishing (KDP) Hardback Cover (optional)

KDP currently offers very limited hardback sizes—5.5" x 8.5", 6" x 9", 6.14" x 9.21", 7" x 10", and 8.25" x 11". Front cover, back cover, and spine PDF for Kindle Direct Publishing. Your cover designer will need to follow the Kindle Direct Publishing cover submission guidelines.

8. Kindle Direct Publishing (KDP) Hardback Interior (optional)

Interior PDF for Kindle Direct Publishing. Your formatter will need to follow the Kindle Direct Publishing interior submission guidelines.

9. Cover Local Printer (optional)

You may choose this option if you'd like to do a larger print run (higher upfront cost but lower cost per unit). Also, local printers may offer more paper options than what IngramSpark or KDP provide, as well as specialty printing features such as foiling, embossing, debossing, and spot UV that give your book that special X-factor.

You will need the PDF files for the front cover, back cover, and spine for any local or offshore printer with whom you decide to do business. Your cover designer can use the IngramSpark paperback file but will need to liaise with your local printer to ensure they adhere to the right specs.

10. Interior Local Printer (optional)

Interior PDF for any local or offshore printer with whom you decide to do business. Your typesetter can use the IngramSpark paperback interior file but will need to liaise with your printer.

Files You Will Need for Your E-Book

Before you order your e-book files, please ensure that you read the *Publish Your E-book* section in the *Publish* chapter to learn about the pros and cons of publishing your e-book solely on KDP versus publishing "wide" via IngramSpark and KDP.

I would not recommend trying to format your e-book yourself. Books that aren't correctly formatted may result in your book being rejected by Amazon, in readers posting negative comments on your Amazon page, and poor sales. You can ask your graphic designer who does the print book typesetting/layout to convert the final files to an e-book for KDP and IngramSpark once all edits are complete. Or you can hire a separate professional e-book formatter from Upwork. com* or Fiverr.com*. Here is a link to Upwork*: https://upwork.pxf. io/c/347458/1062918/13634. Here is a link to Fiverr*: https://fvrr. co/2SxlAAV. The beauty of hiring a professional is that you won't have to worry about either publishing platform rejecting your files.

Also, typically, when files are done appropriately by a professional, they will include some digital copyright protections/encryptions as well. By uploading a simple or poorly formatted file to Amazon, a writer runs the risk of having pirates download their e-book, remove their name and identifying information, and reprinting/plagiarizing their work as well.

KDP recommends uploading a Kindle Package Format (KPF) file and IngramSpark supports an ePub file when publishing your e-book. KDP says KPF files allow your e-book to fit all Kindle devices, and avoid any formatting issues. It comes in both reflowable and fixed formats. The ePub format is the globally accepted format for e-books and can be read on every e-reader. The format is reflowable.

The quote from e-book formatter will depend on the length of your book, whether your book is a simple novel with all text and no pictures or whether it has tables and graphics in it and how many. It will also depend on whether you'd like it in black and white and standard reflowable text or whether you'd like it in color and in fixed layout. Novels are better in standard reflowable format. Fixed format is great for books that rely heavily on images and artistic layouts such as children's books, cookbooks, health and fitness books, journals, and travel guides.

The formatter will then convert your book to a KPF and/or ePub file—complete with a hyperlinked Table of Contents for a nonfiction book, which means your readers will be able to jump straight to a particular chapter simply by clicking on that chapter's heading rather than scrolling through the entire book. It will also have any other hyperlinks to your website or other websites you'd like in your book. Internal links are not supported in fixed layout books.

E-book formatting isn't expensive. For the past few years, I've used the services of a professional e-book converter who, depending on the complexity of the project, converts the InDesign files of your paperback book to KPF and ePub format plus e-book front cover for both KDP and IngramSpark for approximately US$90 for both files within three days.

Although your e-book converter can convert your PDF, it's easier and more cost effective to send the packaged InDesign files. Give the designer the IngramSpark paperback cover and interior PDFs, too, for quality control.

Please note if your book is a standard flowable format for a novel or nonfiction book, the formatters will strip out any of the pretty fonts you used in your MS Word document, and you'll be left with a basic font such as Georgia, Caecilia, Trebuchet, Verdana, Arial, Times New Roman, Courier, or Lucida. Readers will have the ability to set the font they prefer to read on their Kindle or other e-reader devices.

STEPS TO ORDERING YOUR E-BOOKS

1. Negotiate with your book formatter to convert your book to a KPF file for KDP and an ePub file if you are publishing outside KDP. Or find a specialist e-book converter from Upwork.com* or Fiverr.com* to do the e-book conversions for you. Here is a link to Upwork*: https://upwork.pxf.io/c/347458/1062918/13634. Here is a link to Fiverr*: https://fvrr.co/2SxlAAV.

2. If you are hiring a separate e-book formatter, ask your cover designer and typesetter to send you the packaged InDesign files plus the IngramSpark PDFs of your paperback book (for quality control) via a file-sharing software like Wetransfer.com. Send these files to the e-book converter to receive a quote.

3. If you are happy with the quote, ask them to convert your print book files into two e-book file formats (a KPF and an e-Pub file).

4. There is another option for IngramSpark. You can simply click *Convert to e-book* on IngramSpark and convert your IngramSpark paperback straight to an e-book. The process takes about 15 days and costs US$0.60 per page. If you don't want to wait that long, simply pay an e-book converter.

Files You Will Receive from the E-Book Converter:

1. **KPF File and ePub File**—E-book file for KDP and IngramSpark.

2. **Front Cover**—Front cover JPEG for KDP and IngramSpark.

COVER REQUIREMENTS FOR
YOUR E-BOOK FRONT COVER

Below is a summary of the cover required by KDP and IngramSpark for you to give your e-book converter.

❧ Your cover will need to be a JPEG file.

❧ In terms of size, your image needs to be a minimum of 625 pixels on the shortest side and 1,000 pixels on the longest side.

❧ For best quality, your image will be 1,563 pixels on the shortest side and 2,500 pixels on the longest side.

❧ Images display on the Amazon website using RGB (red, green, blue) color mode. Make sure you use a color image.

#GENIUS TIP!

Before you request your e-book files, publish your IngramSpark paperback book. Once you have read through your printed sample and are happy with it, then get your e-book files done. If you do your e-book before you have read the printed sample, you'll have to make changes to *all* files if you pick up any errors in the printed sample, which will cost you more.

Self-Publishing Success Story—T. S. Paul

T. S. Paul (aka Scott Paul) started writing short fiction in 2016. His first book, *The Forgotten Engineer*, received negative reviews for poor writing, bad grammar, and typos, but the more he wrote, the more he improved. He tried several different genres—science fiction, space opera, military, light horror, and paranormal fiction books, releasing new e-books every few weeks. Within four months, he was selling thousands of e-books. He has no author website and no mailing list, merely a blog and a Facebook page where he runs ads to build awareness of his books. He releases a new book every month, all of which are under 100 pages and an average word count of 10,000 words. These are free for 24 hours. Thereafter, there is a Buy Now button where you can buy the e-book on any retailer for US$1.99 and a pre-order button for the next in the series. Within a couple of years, he became a six-figure author (Leslie 2018).

"Genius is 1 percent inspiration, 99 percent perspiration."

—Thomas A. Edison, prolific inventor and author of
The Diary and Sundry Observations of Thomas Alva Edison

It's time to publish your books! Woohoo!

CHECKING IN

Congratulations on getting this far! It takes a lot of commitment and dedication to get to this point. It's time to check in to see how you're doing.

What have you accomplished so far?

_____

_____

_____

_____

_____

What have been your biggest disappointments?

_____

_____

_____

_____

What have you observed about yourself?

_____

_____

_____

_____

_____

What new insights have you gained?

_____

_____

_____

_____

What important breakthroughs have you made?

_____

_____

_____

_____

What new habits are you practicing?

_____

_____

_____

_____

What has been the most fun?

_____

_____

_____

What important new challenges are you facing?

_____

_____

_____

_____

What new opportunities have emerged?

_____

_____

_____

_____

What can you say to yourself to help you get across the finish line?

_____

_____

_____

_____

What is the most important next step?

_____

_____

_____

_____

What specific commitments will you make?

_____

_____

_____

_____

My gift to myself for doing the hard work will be:

_____

_____

_____

"Courage starts with showing up and letting ourselves be seen."

—Brené Brown, author of *Daring Greatly, Rising Strong, The Gifts of Imperfection, Dare to Lead, Braving the Wilderness* and *Atlas of the Heart*

7.

PUBLISH

"I finished my first book seventy-six years ago. I offered it to every publisher on the English-speaking earth I had ever heard of. Their refusals were unanimous: and it did not get into print until, fifty years later; publishers would publish anything that had my name on it."

—George Bernard Shaw, Irish playwright

If you have arrived at this chapter, then congratulations! I know you are serious and ready to go the distance. Here I'll present to you up-to-date industry knowledge of the changing landscape of independent publishing with the intention of guiding you through the process of successfully birthing your book into the world.

We'll look at the benefits of having a book in print on IngramSpark and Kindle Direct Publishing. We will also discuss what's involved when publishing an e-book, including making the decision to go exclusive to KDP or "wide." It's also time to talk money—the cost of printing and setting the correct price for your book. These are rich and rewarding conversations with decisions to be made that will set the tone of your book's life on the market, so be sure to set aside uninterrupted time to wrap your head around each section.

But first, let's revisit the 10 reasons why self-publishing is so compelling:

1. Your chance of being published by a mainstream publisher is about 1%–2% (Talbot 2023).

2. If you get accepted by a mainstream publisher, the average time from acceptance to bookshelf sales is 18 months.

3. Self-publishing sidesteps rejection letters and blows to your self-esteem. Instead, you can focus on building your author platform from the get-go.

4. You will bypass mainstream publishers and share your brilliance with the world, gain credibility, and earn money from your writing straight away.

5. More profit in your pocket. With a mainstream publisher, royalties average 6%–10% of net receipts. When you sell directly to your audience from your website or at events, you keep 100%. If you sell on Amazon, you'll earn between 35 and 70%. If you sell through a distributor, you'll get to keep 31.5%.

6. You have full control over your words, cover design, formatting, pricing—everything! You retain all rights to your book and oversee the entire publishing process. Updates can be made over time to improve the book, so it evolves with you and your vision.

7. There's a whole world of creative professionals available online to collaborate with you! Editors, ghostwriters, cover designers, typesetters, and e-book converters, as well as publishing, printing, and distribution platforms, are just a Google search away, ready and willing to help produce your book.

8. Due to technological advances, self-publishing achieves the same high-quality printing and book distribution once reserved for traditionally published authors.

9. Print-on-demand (POD) ensures affordability for the author and sustainability for the environment. You can print one or 1,000 books, depending on your plans for distribution.

10. Your chances of engagement with a mainstream publisher are greater with a self-published book to your name. Richard Paul Evans took six weeks to write the 87-page *The Christmas Box*. He self-published it, sold it to family and friends, and then watched it soar. Mainstream publishing house Simon & Schuster caught wind of his success and paid him $4.2 million for it!

Are you ready to delve deep into the details to get your self-published book show on the road?

Rejected by Mainstream Publishers

- J. K. Rowling, *Harry Potter*—12 times
- Norman Mailer, *The Naked and the Dead*—12 times
- Richard Bach, *Jonathan Livingstone Seagull*—20 times
- Alex Haley—200 rejections before *Roots*
- Robert Pirsig, *Zen and the Art of Motorcycle Maintenance*—121 times
- John Grisham, *A Time to Kill*—15 publishers and 30 agents (he ended up self-publishing it)
- *Chicken Soup for the Soul*—144 times
- Dr. Seuss—24 times
- Jack London—600 rejections before his first story
- John Creasy—774 rejections before selling his first story. He went on to write 564 books using 14 names
- Stephen King's first four novels were rejected
- Amanda Hocking—1,000 rejections before self-publishing her first vampire novel

SELF-PUBLISHING USED TO HAVE A STIGMA—BUT NO MORE!

Even traditionally published authors are moving away from publishers and doing it themselves. J. K. Rowling now sells the e-book versions of her Harry Potter series from her own site, Pottermore.com.

"I hope you figure out that each day you don't self-publish is a day you could have earned money but didn't. That's the bottom line, gang!"

—J. A. Konrath, bestselling author in the horror, thriller, and comedy genre who received 500 rejection letters from mainstream publishers.

He has now sold more than 4 million books worldwide.

Five Reasons Why You Need to Have a Printed Book as an Author

1. A printed book still holds way more credibility than an e-book.

2. There is more perceived value in a printed book than an e-book.

3. People will pay more for a printed book than an e-book.

4. It may come as a surprise, but readers prefer printed books over e-books. A Gallup study showed that 73% of people prefer reading printed books to e-books (Library Research Service 2021).

5. Printed books will continue to outsell e-books. The global paper books market will encompass around 1.87 billion readers by 2027, while e-reader users are expected to reach 1.2 billion (Errera 2023). So make sure you have both a printed version and an e-book version available to your readers!

Why You Absolutely Need to Make Your Book Available on Amazon

- Amazon is the largest seller of books in the world. It operates 21 online websites worldwide, including websites in United States, Canada, Mexico, United Kingdom, Germany, France, Italy, Spain, Japan, Singapore, United Arab Emirates, Brazil, Australia, India, Netherlands, Saudi Arabia, Turkey, Sweden, Poland, Belgium, and Egypt.

- Amazon earns an estimated US$28 billion a year from selling books and takes more than 50%–80% of the market share of book sales (Vanheesan and Pincok 2024).

- By making your book available on Amazon (paperback, hardback, e-book, and/or audio), you can take advantage of

Amazon's programs and features that will expose your book to millions of eyeballs around the world. These include KDP Select, KU (Kindle Unlimited), Amazon ads, and Amazon recommendations features such as *Customers Who Bought This Book Also Bought*. More on this later.

Benefits of Publishing on Both IngramSpark and Kindle Direct Publishing

I recommend publishing on both IngramSpark and Kindle Direct Publishing because they have different benefits.

INGRAMSPARK

- **Global distribution:** Your book will be made available to millions of potential customers around the world via the largest global distribution networks, including 40,000 libraries and retailers such as Amazon, Barnes & Noble, and Waterstones. You'll find a full list on the IngramSpark website here: https://www.ingramspark.com/how-it-works/distribute.

- **Faster print on demand:** You can print on demand between one and 3,000 books whenever you want, and they are delivered to you within 1–5 days. You can print on-demand author copies from KDP, but they take 1–2 weeks and sometimes longer to arrive. You can order books that are delivered within 1–2 days from KDP, but only if you pay the retail price and your book needs to be live. Most other specialist book printers require a minimum order of 300 to 1,000 copies.

- **More printing options:** There is a greater range of paper options than on KDP, as well as more hardcover sizes and options, which includes publishing a hardcover with a dust jacket.

KDP

- **Better royalties with KDP:** Your royalties will be better overall with KDP. Amazon owns KDP, so it makes it easier for customers to buy your KDP book over your IngramSpark book. It costs less to print and gives you higher royalties. For example, with a 6"x9" paperback priced at US$14.99 with a 40% discount, the print cost is US$4.08 for IngramSpark compared with US$3.40 for KDP, and the royalty is US$4.76 for IngramSpark compared to US$5.59 for KDP.

- **Amazon ads:** KDP gives you the opportunity to run ads on Amazon.com or your preferred Amazon site, which provides lots of exposure and increased sales.

- **You'll get paid for Pages Read:** Enrolling your e-book in KDP Select allows you to get paid for pages read when Amazon subscribers download your e-book through its Kindle Unlimited program. This can bring in a really good income over time. (More on Kindle Unlimited on page 244).

- **Clear *Read Sample (Look Inside the Book)* feature:** It gives you a clear *Read Sample* feature when customers click on your cover on Amazon, which gives them the opportunity to see the content inside your book. That is not always the case if you enable the *Look Inside* feature on IngramSpark, in my experience.

GET MY STEP-BY-STEP PUBLISHING CHECKLIST

Before you begin your publishing journey, you may wish to download my simple Publishing Checklist, which lists the exact steps I use to publish my own clients' books. Download it at iinspiremedia.com.au.

"Nothing stinks like a pile of unpublished writing."

—Sylvia Plath, author of *The Bell Jar*

Publish Your Paperback and/or Hardback Book on IngramSpark

You'll have the ability to create the most beautiful paperback and/or hardback book on IngramSpark. Paperback books are most common for fiction and nonfiction. Hardbacks are more expensive to produce than a paperback, but you can charge more. You can print your children's book, cookbook, family memoir, or workbook in hardback, setting up and offering both versions at different price points if you so desire (e.g., charge US$19.95 for the paperback and US$29.95 for the hardback).

Here are the steps to publishing your book on IngramSpark.

HAVE YOUR PDF FILES BEFORE YOU START

Before you start it's a good idea to have the correct IngramSpark paperback cover PDF from your cover designer and your paperback interior PDF from your typesetter. These have been created according to the IngramSpark submission guidelines (Please read the previous chapter on *Layout*.) Make sure you that your barcode on your back cover matches the ISBN on the imprint page.

CREATE AN ACCOUNT ON INGRAMSPARK

Use your email address and create a unique password. When you log on the first time, you'll be required to sign various agreements, including the Global POD Agreement, the Global E-Book Agreement and the Apple E-Book Agreement. I recommend accepting all agreements except for the Amazon (Kindle) E-Book Agreement. This is so you will be able to upload your e-book directly onto Kindle Direct Publishing and get the benefits of your e-book being on KDP. Complete the areas for your bank or PayPal account, publisher, tax, and credit card information so you'll receive royalties.

SET UP YOUR PRINTED BOOK

Select *Add Title* on your Dashboard. Then select *Print Book Only*. It is best to set up your paperback book first so that you can order a sample and check it thoroughly before you do any other versions. If you select *Print & E-Book*, you'll need the cover and interior PDFs, ePub, and the JPG cover image all at the same time. Then if you order the printed version and you need to make changes, you'll have to make changes to the e-book as well.

IngramSpark will then ask you "Do you have files ready to upload?" Click *No, But I Will Enter My Title Information and Submit Files Later*. To the next question, "What would you like to do?" please select *Print, Distribute and Sell Book*.

COMPLETE ALL INFORMATION FOR YOUR BOOK

This is called the "metadata" and conveys information about your book to customers, bookstores, and libraries. Complete the following fields:

TITLE INFORMATION

- **Title.** You will have chosen this based on your keyword research (See *The Amazon Algorithm* in the *Plan* chapter). Ideally you will have your main keyword in your title, preferably at the beginning, which will help with your Amazon ranking. E.g., *Podcasting for Entrepreneurs*.

- **Language.** Identify in which language the book is written.

- **Print ISBN.** This is for your paperback book printed by IngramSpark. You'll need a different one if you do a hardback version, ePub version, and for your KDP paperback version.

- **Publishing Rights.** Select *I Own the Copyright or Hold Necessary Publishing Rights*.

- **Artificial Intelligence.** Has AI been used in the creation of this work? Select *Yes* or *No*. If you have used AI to help generate content, then select *Yes* and then select *Text, Images and/or Editorial Function* and specify how you have used it.

Click *Show More Fields to Improve Book Optimization.*

- **Book Subtitle.** This will contain your researched keywords and help potential customers know what your book is about to eliminate any confusion. (e.g., *A Children's Book about Developing Resilience* or *A Gripping Science Fiction Novel*).

- **Series Name and Number (optional).** Enter this information if your book is part of a series. Be strategic and use the most searched keywords within your series name. (e.g., if you have a series of children's books about mental health and resilience, and you determine on Publisher Rocket° that there are more than 1,000 searches per month on Amazon for the keywords *mental health kids*, with medium to low competition, then call your series name *Mental Health for Kids*.)

- **Edition Number (optional).** Leave this blank unless you've made significant changes to the first edition then you can call it a second edition.

AUTHORS & CONTRIBUTORS

- **Contributor #1.** Select *Author* under Role on the dropdown menu. Enter your author name.

Click *Show More Fields to Improve Book Optimization.*

- **Contributor Biography.** Enter your short author bio.

- **Contributor Prior Work.** Enter any prior books you have written.

If you have a children's book, click *Add a Contributor* and add the name of your illustrator and your illustrator's short author bio.

CATEGORIZE YOUR TITLE

- **Select Imprint.** Insert your publishing name. If you don't find it in the dropdown menu, select *Add Imprint* and add it in.

- **Subjects.** Click *Find Subjects* and type in a simple one-word term such as *Parenting* or *Dogs* which will then generate a list of possible genres. Select up to three of the most suitable subject categories in which your book belongs by clicking each category and selecting *Add Subject*. Try to avoid general categories if you can. It's better to niche your book into one of the smaller categories so your book has more of a chance of being found and ranking at the top of that category.

  1. Books > Health, Fitness & Dieting > Diseases & Physical Ailments > Sleep Disorders

  2. Books > Health, Fitness & Dieting > Psychology & Counseling > Child Psychology

  3. Books > Parenting & Relationships > Parenting > Early Childhood

  If you have Publisher Rocket*, go to *Category Search*, where you can choose the best categories for your book, or click on *Competition Analyzer*, then see which books are doing well in your genre, and click on *See the Categories* to get a good idea of what categories would be suitable for your own book. Here's a link to Publisher Rocket*: https://iinspiremedia--rocket.thrivecart. com/publisher-rocket/

- **Select Audience.** If you are not choosing a particular age range such as Juvenile (0–12) or Young Adult (13–18), it is best to choose Trade/General (Adult) here.

  Click *Show More Fields to Improve Book Optimization.*

- **Thema Subjects.** Click *Find Subjects* and choose as many relevant subjects as you can fit here to categorize your book.

- **Table of Contents.** Cut and paste your final table of contents from your book's interior into this section. Do not include page numbers.

- **Review Quotes.** Include several testimonials that you've collected in this section to provide social proof. Brief excerpts of the full quote are more impactful.

TITLE DESCRIPTION

- **Full Description.** Include up to 4,000 bytes (approximately 600 words) describing what the book is about. This is what will appear on book retail websites to encourage customers to buy your book. You can use your back cover blurb. Make sure you optimize your book description by sprinkling keywords throughout. This will help your rankings on Amazon and other book retail sites.

- **Keywords.** Enter between 10–20 keywords and phrases, separated by semicolons, that potential buyers may be searching for in book retailer and Google search engines such as *Mediterranean diet, substance abuse,* or *self-help books for women.* There is a great article on keywords to choose here: https://kindlepreneur.com/7-kindle-keywords/. To find keywords for your book, you can do accurate research on Publisher Rocket*. https://iinspiremedia--rocket.thrivecart.com/publisher-rocket/

  In addition, if you start typing your keywords into the Amazon search bar, it will prompt you with the most commonly typed-in applicable keywords and phrases that you may use here.

  Click *Show More Fields to Improve Book Optimization.*

- **Short Description.** Tell the book retailers about your book in just one or two sentences (250 bytes or about 30–35 words).

  Click *Continue* to move to the next page.

PRINT INFORMATION

- **Select Trim Size.** Select the book size that you chose with your cover designer and book formatter. (See a list of recommended book sizes under *Layout* on page 189).

- **Interior Color and Paper.** Will you be printing the interior in black-and-white or color? If you choose black-and-white, will you choose white 50, white 70, cream 50, or groundwood 38 eggshell paper? White is used more for nonfiction books. Cream is commonly used for fiction. Groundwood is more for mass-market fiction. If you choose color, then you can choose standard 50, standard 70, premium color, or ultra-premium color. Premium color should be used for children's books, travel books, and cookbooks. Ultra-premium color is ideal for photography books, coffee table books, and high-quality children's books. The higher the quality paper, the higher the cost to print your book. See *How Much Does It Cost to Print a Book* on page 228.

- **Binding.** Select *Paperback* and *Perfect Bound*, a glued spine with a color cover and the normal binding for paperback books.

  Once your paperback version is set up, you'll be able to create a hardcover version simply by selecting *Duplicate* from the dropdown menu under Actions on the Dashboard. All the metadata from your paperback book will be copied over and you'll simply need to add in a new ISBN and choose your hardcover specs.

  Select *Hardback,* and then choose one of the following: *Case Laminate* (color laminated cover glued to boards, no dust jacket), *Digital Cloth Cover—Blue* (with or without dust jacket, text printed on spine), or *Digital Cloth Cover—Gray* (with or without dust jacket, text printed on spine), or *Jacketed Case Laminate* (color laminated cover glued to boards with dust jacket).

Book Binding Types for Your Cover

Perfect bound—Pages and paperback cover glued together at spine.

Case laminate—Pages glued to hardcover at ends for a hardback book.

Jacketed case laminate—Pages glued to hardcover at ends with the option to design what prints on the cover beneath the jacket.

🙢 **Cover Finish.** For your paperback book, you can choose a gloss or a matte cover, depending on your personal preference. For your hardback cover, you can choose a gloss or a matte cover on case laminate or with a dust jacket. You can also choose a textured feel if you choose digital cloth with no dust jacket, which means that you can feel the lettering on the cover.

Book Cover Textures

Matte cover—Soft feel, no glare, polished.

Gloss cover—High shine, smooth finish.

Digital cloth cover—Subtle, clothlike look (available with or without dust jacket). Textured feel is available with this option.

ADDITIONAL BOOK INFORMATION

- **Duplex Enabled.** Select *Yes* if your inside cover is printed or *No* if your inside cover is blank. Duplex covers are only available for perfect bound books in limited sizes. If you select this option, ensure your book formatter has given you the appropriate duplex files; there is an additional print cost.

- **Page Count.** Enter the number of pages inside your book (do not include the cover). When you open your interior PDF file, you'll see the number of pages on the file.

PRINT PRICING

- **Retail Price.** Make sure you look at a variety of bookstores online and price your book competitively with others in your genre. Use a currency converter to convert for all currencies and make all prices end in ".99" or ".95," as these are tried-and-tested pricing strategies. You will find, for example, that books are cheaper on Amazon.com than they are in Australian bookstores, so take that into account when you price your book. Also, Amazon.com will slash the price after a few days as a marketing strategy. Amazon.com.au, on the other hand, tends to increase your AUD price by A$5–$20, so you will need to keep an eye on the price once it's published on Amazon.com.au. If the price it too high when it goes live, you'll have to reduce it on the IngramSpark pricing dashboard.

- **Wholesale Discount and Returns.** Choose between 40% and 55% as a retail discount and select *Yes* or *No* to returns. IngramSpark recommends that you select 55% and make it returnable if your goal is to be in bookstores because that alleviates the bookstore's risk and makes your book similar to those offered to them by traditional publishers. However, most of my clients find that 55% leaves them with a close to negative royalty, and they are reluctant to leave themselves open to the risk of having to pay for hundreds of books being returned to them. If your goal is online sales, you can simply select a 40% discount and say *No* to returns.

Tick the box saying *I Accept All Prices Above.*

PRINT OPTIONS

- **Enable Look Inside the Book.** I would not tick *Enable Look Inside the Book*, as KDP has a better *Read Sample* feature and because your KDP paperback will go live first, this will be used.

- **Large Text Edition.** Only tick this box if your book is a large text edition.

- **Right-to-Left Content.** Do not select this box unless your content is meant to be bound and read in reverse.

PRINT RELEASE DATES

- **Publication Date.** This is the official release date of your book. Put a date in the future that gives you enough time to order a sample, make corrections and upload revised versions of your book.

- **On-Sale Date.** This is the date that retailers are allowed to sell your book. I always update these dates to the current date once I'm happy with the book and ready to enable the book for global distribution.

Click *Continue* to move to the next page.

UPLOAD YOUR PRINT INTERIOR AND PRINT COVER FILES

Select and upload your IngramSpark print interior PDF and your print cover PDF files and click *Continue*. The files will process and will let you know whether or not there are issues. Please email any issues to your book formatter to fix. They will send you revised files to upload. If there are no issues, you'll receive a message on the Dashboard letting you know that you will receive an email from IngramSpark in three to five days, asking you to approve the e-proof and to order a sample.

APPROVE FOR PRINT

You will receive an email from IngramSpark that your proof is ready to approve. Log in to your IngramSpark account and find your book. Click *Approve*, and you will be taken to a screen to download your proof. Check your proof. Approve it for print from your account only.

ORDER A PRINTED SAMPLE

Go to your Dashboard and click *Place Order* for one book. Choose the fastest printing and fastest, safest shipping method. You may have to select *Override on Sale Date* if your publication date is in the future, otherwise you won't receive your sample.

When you receive your sample in the mail, check it thoroughly. If there are any edits you'd like to make, create a list of changes and send these to the cover designer and/or formatter. They will make the changes and send you revised files. You will then have to upload the revised files and once again submit them for review. When IngramSpark has approved the revised files, you'll need to approve the e-proof again and order another sample. Remember, you can only order your book if you have approved the IngramSpark e-proof for print.

ENABLE FOR GLOBAL DISTRIBUTION

I recommend enabling your book for distribution *only after* your KDP book is live on Amazon and the *Read Sample* feature on your KDP book is showing (see *Publish Your Paperback and/or Hardback Book on Kindle Direct Publishing* on page 230).

IngramSpark takes up to 15 days for your book and all its metadata to appear across all book retailers globally. If the book cover image or some of its metadata is still not showing up after 15 days, please contact IngramSpark, and they will alert the bookstore.

Your books are now for sale across all retailers globally and can be purchased by customers around the world. You can also order as many books as you wish from your Dashboard, and you have the option of shipping full orders to retailers and individuals to customers.

INGRAMSPARK PUBLISHING CHECKLIST

I have set up all my account, publisher, tax, and credit card information on IngramSpark so I can order books as well as get paid royalties at the reduced tax rate: Yes ☐ No ☐

My book has been correctly formatted for IngramSpark: Yes ☐ No ☐

Title: _____

Subtitle: _____

Short Description (approximately 35 words):

_____

_____

_____

_____

_____

Full Description (approximately 600 words):

_____

_____

_____

_____

_____

_____

_____

_____

_____

_____

_____

_____

_____

_____

_____

_____

Contributors (your author name and the name of your illustrator if you have a children's book):

_____

_____

_____

_____

Author Bio (your short author bio):

_____

_____

_____

_____

_____

_____

_____

_____

_____

_____

_____

_____

_____

_____

Keywords (around 10 keywords or phrases):

1. _____

2. _____

3. _____

4. _____

5. _____

6. _____

7. _____

8. _____

9. _____

10. _____

Your Imprint Name (your publishing name):

_____

Subjects (up to three suitable categories for your genre):

_____

_____

_____

_____

ISBN _ _ _ _ _ _ _ _ _ _ _ _ _ (paperback)

ISBN _ _ _ _ _ _ _ _ _ _ _ _ _ (hardback)

Book Size (e.g., 5.5" x 8.5"):

_____

Interior Color (color or black-and-white):

_____

Interior Paper (white or color 50, white or color 70, cream 50, groundwood 38, premium color, or ultra-premium color):

_____

Paperback Cover Finish (gloss or matte):

_____

Hardback Book Binding (case laminate, digital cloth blue or grey with or without dust jacket, or jacketed case laminate):

_____

Hardback Cover Finish (textured, gloss, or matte):

_____

Paperback Pricing:

USD _____

GBP _____

EUR _____

CAD _____

AUD _____

Hardback Pricing:

USD _____

GBP _____

EUR _____

CAD _____

AUD _____

I have approved my e-proof for print and ordered a sample of my paperback book on IngramSpark: Yes ☐ No ☐

I have seen my paperback sample book and sent edits back to the typesetter (if there are edits):   Yes ☐ No ☐

I have seen my paperback sample book and am happy with it!   Yes ☐ No ☐

Now that I'm happy with my IngramSpark paperback sample, I have ordered my hardback book files and KDP paperback book files from my formatter, and my e-book files from my formatter/e-book converter: Yes ☐ No ☐

Now that I've published my KDP paperback book and it is live on Amazon.com, I have enabled my IngramSpark paperback for distribution so readers all over the world can buy it: Yes ☐ No ☐

How Much Does It Cost to Print a Book?

This will depend on the number of pages in your book, and whether it is hardcover or paperback and in black-and-white or color. The more pages your book has, the more you will pay. Hardcover is more expensive than paperback. And color is more expensive than black-and-white.

You can get an estimate of costs from the IngramSpark printing and shipping calculator at https://myaccount.ingramspark.com/Portal/Tools/ShippingCalculator.

You can get an idea of what royalties you will make at https://myaccount.ingramspark.com/Portal/Tools/PubCompCalculator.

How Many Books Do I Print?

You should always order a sample copy before you do a larger print run so you can pick up any typos. Then, once you've approved that, an initial batch of 100–300 books is recommended. You'll find that your readers will give you feedback and may pick up a few typos, which you can then correct for the next print run. It is much more cost-effective printing a smaller print run than having a large quantity sitting in your garage. You can print more once you've sold your first batch.

I am going to print _____ copies
for my first print run of books.

"If I just keep putting one foot in front of the other, it stands to reason that I'm going to get there."

—Rachel Joyce, author of *The Unlikely Pilgrimage of Harold Fry*

Publish Your Paperback and/or Hardback Book on Kindle Direct Publishing

To publish your paperback book on Kindle Direct Publishing, follow these simple steps.

HAVE YOUR PDF FILES BEFORE YOU START

Before you start it's a good idea to have the correct KDP paperback cover PDF from your cover designer and your paperback interior PDF from your typesetter. These have been created according to the KDP submission guidelines (see page 191). Make sure you that your barcode on your back cover matches the ISBN on the imprint page.

CREATE AN ACCOUNT ON KINDLE DIRECT PUBLISHING

Go to https://kdp.amazon.com/self-publishing/signin. If you already have an existing Amazon account, *Sign In* using your email address and password. If you don't have an Amazon account, *Sign Up* with an email address and create a password. Agree to the KDP terms and conditions.

COMPLETE YOUR ACCOUNT INFORMATION

If your KDP account is new, the dashboard will state "Your Account Information is Incomplete." Click on *Update Now* and complete your name, address, and bank account details where you would like your royalties to go. Complete the tax interview (this will vary by country).

SET UP YOUR PAPERBACK BOOK FIRST

Once you have signed in or registered on KDP, you'll be taken to the Bookshelf screen. Where it says "Add a New Title," click on *Paperback* to begin the process of creating your paperback book.

COMPLETE ALL THE INFORMATION FOR YOUR BOOK

First, you'll be prompted to enter all your book's details, such as the title, subtitle, book description, keywords, and pricing. This is to help readers find your book in the bookstore. If you've published your IngramSpark paperback, then simply copy and paste all the metadata across from your IngramSpark account for this.

PAPERBACK DETAILS

- **Language.** The language in which you have written your book.

- **Book Title and Subtitle.** Enter the exact title (along with the subtitle) of your book as they appear on your book cover. KDP sometimes reject books if what is on the cover and what is in the title and subtitle metadata do not match. If you do not have a subtitle on your book cover yet, I'd recommend putting one on your cover and adding it into the metadata that contains relevant keywords to help with your rankings on Amazon. For example: *A Children's Book about Developing Resilience.*

- **Series Name and Number (optional).** Enter this information if your book is part of a series (or eventually will be). I usually create a series from the bookshelf later once all books in the series are published. If you create a series, it will build a product page on Amazon, showcasing all your books in the series. Be strategic and use the most searched keywords within your series name.

- **Edition Number (optional).** You can provide an edition number if this title is a new edition of an existing book.

- **Author.** Put in your author name.

- **Contributors.** If you have a coauthor or an illustrator (if you're publishing a children's book), add their name here.

- **Description.** This is what potential readers will see when they see your book on Amazon. It will be the equivalent of the printed book's back cover, so it's got to be engaging and compelling without giving away too much of the story. You have about 600 words to make your book sound so intriguing and captivating that customers feel compelled to click the *Buy Now* button. Make full use of the opportunity of those 600 words for SEO purposes, too, so your book gets found. Scatter your keywords throughout the text in a way that flows naturally. If you can fit them, it's also a clever marketing strategy to add one or two positive reviews you've collected in the lead-up to publishing your book—ideally with keywords!—below your book description for social proof to help your rankings.

  To format your description, you can use the text editor or basic HTML. With the text editor, you can bold, italicize, create lists, and more. These options are available at the top of the Description field. To switch between them, or to check all the characters within your description, you can click on the Source button. To see a list of the supported HTML on Amazon, see https://kdp.amazon.com/en_US/help/topic/G201189630.

- **Publishing Rights.** Click *I Own the Copyright and I Hold Necessary Publishing Rights*. Public domain works refers to those works that belong to authors who have died more than 50–70 years ago (depending on the copyright law in your country) and whose work is now out of copyright and in the public domain.

- **Primary Audience.** Select *Yes* or *No* to whether your book's cover or interior contains sexually explicit images or language. And choose the reading ages (if it's a children's book, a young adult book, or intended for readers 18 and older). If you don't include an appropriate reading age for children, teen, and young adult books, your book may not be eligible for your selected Children's or Teen & Young Adult categories, and it may not show up in age-specific search results in the Amazon store.

- **Primary Marketplace.** Choose the Amazon country where you expect the majority of your book sales.

- **Categories.** Choose up to three categories that most fit the genre of your book. For example:

    1. Books > Reference > Writing, Research & Publishing Guides > Publishing & Books > Authorship

    2. Books > Business & Money > Business Development & Entrepreneurship > Entrepreneurship

    3. Books > Reference > Writing, Research & Publishing Guides > Publishing & Books > Book Industry

    It's important to choose the more niche categories where it will be easier to get to #1 rather than selecting general categories where your book won't have a chance. If you have Publisher Rocket*, go to *Category Search* where you can choose the best categories for your book, or click on *Competition Analyzer,* then see which books are doing well in your genre and click on *See the Categories* to get a good idea of what categories would be most suitable for your own book. Here is the link to Publisher Rocket* https://iinspiremedia--rocket.thrivecart.com/publisher-rocket/

- **Keywords.** Search keywords are typically short phrases that Amazon buyers type into the search bar to help them find a book when they are browsing the site (e.g., *romance suspense books*). Help readers find your book by adding up to seven keywords and phrases that best relate to your book. For example, my book *Breaking the Sound Barriers: 9 Deaf Success Stories* has the following keywords: *books about deaf culture, deaf, parent of deaf child, deaf children, hearing loss, deaf culture*, and *hard of hearing*.

Publisher Rocket* will give you invaluable insights into relevant keywords and phrases for your book: https://iinspiremedia--rocket.thrivecart.com/publisher-rocket/. Alternatively, if you don't have Publisher Rocket*, start typing your keywords into the Amazon search bar, and it will prompt you with the most commonly entered keywords and phrases you can use. Amazon has strict rules about keywords, so please check here before you start: https://kdp.amazon.com/en_US/help/topic/G201298500

- **Publication Date (optional).** If your book has not been published before, select the first option, *Publication Date and Release Date Are the Same.*

- **Release Date.** If you are publishing your book now, then select *Release My Book For Sale Now.* You can schedule a printed book's release up to 90 days in advance, but this is not a preorder. You can schedule a preorder up to a year in advance only for e-books. More details here: https://kdp.amazon.com/en_US/help/topic/GZUV7SNV728WT4QE.

Click *Save and Continue* to move to the next page.

PAPERBACK CONTENT

- **ISBN.** Select *Add Your Own ISBN.* Use the ISBN you selected from Bowker for your book's KDP version and add in your publishing name. There is the option to get a free ISBN from KDP, but I would not advise doing this because if you use their ISBN, Amazon will be listed as the publisher on record, not your own publishing imprint.

- **Print Options.** Select your interior and paper type—whether *Black-and-White Interior with Cream Paper*, or *Black-and-White*

Interior with White Paper, Standard Color Interior with White Paper, or *Premium Color Interior with White Paper.* Select your book's *Trim Size.* Select your *Bleed Settings.* Choose *Bleed* if you have images or illustrations extending to the edge of the page on your PDF. Otherwise select *No Bleed.* Then choose either *Matte* or *Glossy* for your cover. Your graphic designer/formatter will be able to provide you with the answer to any of these questions.

- **Manuscript.** Click *Upload Paperback Manuscript* and search for your KDP interior book PDF file that you received from your typesetter.

- **Book Cover.** Click *Upload a Cover You Already Have* and search for your cover PDF on your computer. Tick the box that says *Check this Box if the Cover You're Uploading Includes a Barcode.*

- **AI-Generated Content.** Amazon defines AI-generated content as text, images, or translations created by an AI-based tool. If you used an AI-based tool to create the actual content (whether text, images, or translations), it is considered "AI-generated," even if you applied substantial edits afterward. Select *Yes* or *No* to this question. If *Yes,* then use the dropdown menu to specify exactly where and how you used AI in the creation of your book.

- **Book Preview.** Click *Launch Previewer* to preview your book. This is a *very important* part of the KDP publishing process, as you get to see what your book will look like before it is printed to ensure it is within the printing margins, etc. If there are any issues showing with your book, you'll need to alert your book formatter, get revised files, and upload them again. Once everything looks good, click *Approve.*

Click *Save and Continue* to move to the next page.

PAPERBACK RIGHTS & PRICING

- ❦ **Territories.** Select All Territories (Worldwide Rights).

- ❦ **Pricing, Royalties, and Distribution.** After researching similar books in your genre on Amazon.com, put in your US price. Price it competitively with other books within your genre. However, you can price it a little higher than other books on Amazon.com, as it is a new book. Amazon tends to slash the initial price after a few days as a marketing strategy, so start a bit higher than you normally would. This price should be the same as the US price you put into IngramSpark. If you used the same ISBN for your paperback version as IngramSpark, don't tick the *Expanded Distribution* box. If you have used a different ISBN than the IngramSpark paperback, tick the *Expanded Distribution* box. Enter the US price into the US box, and the currency converter will automatically convert for the other Amazon marketplaces. Ensure your prices end in ".99" or ".95" as this is a tried-and-tested psychological pricing strategy that companies have used for years to sell more products.

REQUEST A BOOK PROOF

Before your book goes live, you can order a proof copy, but this can take 1–2 weeks, and sometimes longer, to arrive. Once your book goes live, you can order an author copy from your dashboard (1–2 weeks to arrive) or order as a customer, which takes a couple of days to arrive. As you have already ordered a sample from IngramSpark and made all the edits you want to your book, I'd recommend skipping this step and ordering a copy as a customer once your book is live.

PUBLISH YOUR PAPERBACK BOOK

Click *Publish Your Paperback Book*. Congratulations! You have completed the publishing process on KDP. It can take up to 72 hours for your book to be available for purchase on Amazon.

Once your paperback book is live and ready for sale (first make sure that others can actually buy your book by buying a copy yourself from your own Amazon store), then promote it as much as possible to try and get to #1 on Amazon in your categories (see page 272). Then, publish your e-book and start the #1 Amazon bestseller campaign of your e-book as soon as your e-book is live. You can also publish your hardback if you have one of the limited five sizes available (see below).

Limited Sizes Available for Hardback Version on KDP

You can now publish a hardcover version on KDP although there are currently only five sizes available (5.5" x 8.5", 6" x 9", 6.14" x 9.21", 7" x 10", and 8.25" x 11"). These are printed as case laminate, meaning that the cover art is printed directly onto the cover. KDP doesn't have an option for dust jackets.

Once you have published your paperback book, you can now request your hardback version from your book formatter. Remember, you'll need a new ISBN on the imprint page and barcode on the back cover.

Go to the KDP Bookshelf where your paperback version is and click *Create Hardcover*. All the information from the paperback will already have been populated from the paperback version. You'll simply need to add in the hardback pricing, upload the new hardback cover and interior, and click *Publish*.

Read Sample (or *Look Inside the Book* Feature)

The *Read Sample* feature allows readers to look inside and preview samples of your book. When you publish a book, this feature is automatically enabled. You will wait one to nine days for the *Read Sample* feature to appear on your book cover image on Amazon. com. The KDP printed version will give you the best impression of the inside of your book. Amazon doesn't give you the option to choose which pages you'd like to show readers; it will automatically show up to the first 20% of the inside of your paperback or hardback. I tend to wait until my *Read Sample* is live before I click *Enable for Distribution* on your IngramSpark paperback and hardback books. It can take between one and 15 days for your books to appear globally across all book retail websites.

KDP PUBLISHING CHECKLIST

I have completed my account, publisher, and tax interview information on Kindle Direct Publishing so I can get paid royalties at the reduced tax rate: Yes ☐ No ☐

My book has been correctly formatted for KDP: Yes ☐ No ☐

Language: _____

Title: _____

Subtitle: _____

Series Name (optional): _____

Series Number (optional):
_____

Edition Number (optional):
_____

Contributors (coauthor or illustrator if you have a children's book):

_____

_____

_____

Book Description (approximately 600 words):

_____

_____

_____

_____

_____

_____

_____

_____

_____

_____

_____

_____

_____

Keywords (up to seven keywords or phrases):

1. _____

2. _____

3. _____

4. _____

5. _____

6. _____

7. _____

Categories (up to three suitable categories for your genre):

1. _____

2. _____

3. _____

Publisher (this is your publishing name):

_____

ISBN _ _ _ _ _ _ _ _ _ _ _ _ _ (paperback)

ISBN _ _ _ _ _ _ _ _ _ _ _ _ _ (hardback)

Ink and Paper Type (black-and-white interior with cream paper, black-and-white interior with white paper, standard color interior with white paper, or premium color interior with white paper):

_____

Trim Size (e.g., 5.5" x 8.5"):

_____

Trim Type   Bleed ☐   No Bleed ☐

Paperback Cover Finish   Gloss ☐   Matte ☐

I have the correct KDP cover and interior PDF files   Yes ☐   No ☐
from my cover designer and typesetter:

I have previewed and approved my book or sent any   Yes ☐   No ☐
issues back to the cover designer and/or typesetter:

Paperback Pricing:	Hardback Pricing:
USD	USD
GBP	GBP
EUR	EUR
CAD	CAD
AUD	AUD

I have ordered a copy of my paperback book and am   Yes ☐   No ☐
happy with it!

I am choosing to publish a hardback version on KDP as Yes ☐   No ☐
they have my size available:

"It doesn't matter how many times you get knocked down. All that matters is you get up one more time than you were knocked down."

—Roy T. Bennett, author of *The Light in the Heart*

Publish Your E-Book

If you are serious about maximizing your reach as an author, you will need to offer your readers an e-book version. Even if you personally would never read an e-book, there are millions of readers who do.

SEVEN REASONS WHY READERS LIKE TO READ E-BOOKS

1. You can download e-books instantly.

2. E-books are lighter. You can carry 2,000 e-books on your portable e-reader.

3. They are cheaper than printed books.

4. You can customize the font size in e-books.

5. You can find millions of titles, including niche titles, from an online bookstore, and download them wherever you are without having to go searching for a particular book in numerous bookstores.

6. They are more environmentally friendly than printed books.

7. You can read e-books in the dark while your partner is sleeping.

WHY YOU NEED TO PUBLISH *BOTH* AN E-BOOK AND A PRINT BOOK

You may want to publish your book just as an e-book without doing a paperback version. While this is a quicker, less costly way of publishing, I would highly recommend creating a paperback as well as an e-book version of your book. First, there is far less credibility in being an e-book author rather than an author of a paperback. Giving someone a printed copy of your book holds way more authority than simply sending someone a link to your e-book.

Second, not all your readers want to read your book as an e-book; some may prefer your paperback or even a hardback version. You're already doing so much of the same setup work—putting your book into the book template, getting your book professionally edited, and getting a professional cover designed. It is so worth taking that extra step and setting up a printed file, which will give you two to three different versions (paperback, hardback, and e-book) at three different price points (US$19.99, US$29.95, and US$9.99, respectively). This will massively pay off for you when you come to marketing your book! Not to mention the absolute thrill of holding your own physical book, seeing it in bookstores, or having friends text you photos of where they've seen your book for sale. Magic!

PUBLISH YOUR E-BOOK ON AMAZON KINDLE DIRECT PUBLISHING

There are three major benefits to publishing your e-book directly to Kindle Direct Publishing.

1. **Amazon Ads.** KDP gives you the opportunity to run ads on Amazon, which can greatly increase your exposure and potential sales for your e-book on the Amazon marketplace you choose.

2. **Kindle Unlimited.** Amazon's Kindle Unlimited (KU) is an e-book subscription for readers. For US$11.99 a month, customers may download millions of e-books and thousands of audiobooks from the KU program. If you choose to enroll your e-book in KDP Select, you'll get paid every time someone borrows your book through the KU program and for the number of pages read, which can bring in a good income. But you must be enrolled in KDP Select, which means you must make your e-book exclusive to Amazon for 90 days. (More on KDP Select on page 250).

3. **Amazon Recommendations.** If your book is enrolled in KDP Select, you'll get the benefit of built-in marketing features such

as *Customers Who Bought This Item Also Bought This Book* that help fuel the sales of your book. If you aren't enrolled in KDP Select, Amazon doesn't tend to be as kind to you with their marketing features. (Read more about KDP Select on page 250).

PUBLISH YOUR E-BOOK ON KINDLE DIRECT PUBLISHING

The following steps assume that you already have your printed version on Kindle Direct Publishing, and you have set up your account, tax information, and metadata for your printed book.

HAVE YOUR E-BOOK FILES BEFORE YOU START

Before you start it's a good idea to have the correct KPF or ePub files plus your front cover JPEG from your e-book converter. These have been created according to the KDP submission guidelines. (Please see page 195.)

LOG IN TO YOUR KDP ACCOUNT

Go to Amazon Kindle Direct Publishing at https://kdp.amazon.com/en_US/ and log on using your Amazon email and password.

SET UP YOUR E-BOOK

Click *Create Kindle E-Book* next to your paperback version on the Bookshelf. It will use all your existing details that you entered for your paperback book, including title, subtitle, the language in which you wrote the book, series and edition number (if you have those), author, other contributors, book description, publishing rights, primary marketplace, keywords, and age range. Read through all the metadata and make sure you are happy with it. Then complete all remaining information for your e-book.

KINDLE E-BOOK DETAILS

- ❧ **Categories.** Choose up to three categories based on your primary marketplace. Get some help from Publisher Rocket* to choose niche categories in which you can actually get to #1. https://iinspiremedia--rocket.thrivecart.com/publisher-rocket/.

- ❧ **Preorder.** You have two options here:

  1. **Make My E-Book Available for Preorder:** Amazon allows you the opportunity to list your e-book for preorder up to a year before its release date. Customers who preordered your e-book will have it automatically delivered to their Kindle. You must upload your e-book 72 hours prior to the release date, otherwise your preorder will be cancelled, and Amazon will ban you from doing a preorder of any other e-book for a year.

  2. **I Am Ready to Release My Book Now:** Choose this option once you've received your KPF or ePub file from an e-book converter from Upwork* or Fiverr.com*. Click *I Am Ready to Release My Book Now.*

Click *Save and Continue* to move to the next page.

KINDLE E-BOOK CONTENT

- ❧ **Manuscript.** Before you upload your e-book file, KDP asks whether or not you'd like to enable digital rights management (DRM).

To DRM or Not to DRM? That Is the Question!

This question always causes the most controversy among my clients and students.

Digital rights management, or DRM, is software designed to prevent sharing. If you click *Enable Digital Rights Management*, it means buyers will find it very difficult to share your book with others or to use the book on different devices.

It sounds great in theory—DRM protects you, the author, from other people stealing your work. Some authors believe DRM is essential to prevent copyright infringement, and it also helps your continued revenue streams by encouraging people to buy, rather than share, your work.

However, DRM limits what you can do with an e-book and where you can send your files. It's annoying for users who pay for your book and like it so much they want to share your book with others (or would like to transfer it to other devices). Once you enable it, you cannot go back and disable it. You have one opportunity—one chance to get it right!

The first option allows you to share your book with others for a short period. The second option allows the buyer to share it with others for unlimited periods. It also allows readers to read your book across multiple devices.

Here is my belief on this one after reading many forums on the issue:

Don't make it hard for your readers! Click *Do Not Enable Digital Rights Management.* Just like they would have done with a printed book, allow them to share your Kindle book and to enjoy your book on whichever devices they prefer.

People who don't know about you will be able to discover your work if their friends have shared your Kindle book with them and will then look for your other titles. If your primary aim as a new author is to get more exposure, more eyeballs on your work, and more readers, then don't enable DRM. Pirates who are going to steal your e-book can disable DRM easily anyway.

Now that's out of the way, let's upload your book!

Click *Upload Manuscript* and browse for your KPF or ePub file that you received from your e-book formatter on your computer. Amazon currently recommends using a KPF file. Click *Open*. Click the *Upload E-Book* button.

ॐ **Kindle E-Book Cover.** Assuming you have your JPEG cover file on your desktop, click *Upload a Cover You Already Have*, locate your Kindle cover file, and then click *Open Your Cover File*. This should successfully upload your image.

You'll need to wait a few minutes while KDP converts your book. If everything is okay with your book, you'll see the message *Upload and Conversion Successful* on your screen. This is when you can do a happy dance!

You may also get a message that states, *Several Issues Have Been Found with Your File—Click Here to View Them*. Clicking this option will lead you to a detailed list of the issues found with your file, and you will then need to have your e-book formatter fix them.

ॐ **AI-Generated Content.** Tick *Yes* or *No* if you used AI tools in creating texts, images, and/or translations in your book.

ॐ **Kindle E-Book Preview.** Previewing your book is a *very important* part of the publishing process. This is where you get to see what your readers will see when they read your book. Click *Preview Book* to preview most books as they will appear on the Kindle, Kindle Fire, iPad, or iPhone. If you want to see your book as it will appear on the Kindle Touch or Kindle DX, click on *Download Previewer* to view your book.

Check your table of contents. Is it hyperlinked to the chapters, and is all the front matter correct? Look for characters that may not have converted correctly. Can you see the photos properly? Are the captions to photos in their correct position under the photo? Do all the hyperlinks work? If your book is correct and will be a great reading experience for your readers, and you are happy with all the details you have entered on the first page, you are ready to move on to the next page. You can then click *Save and Continue* at the bottom of the page.

- **Kindle E-Book ISBN.** You do not need an ISBN to publish on Kindle. Amazon will give you an ASIN number, which stands for Amazon Standard Identification Number and uniquely identifies your book, so leave this form field blank.

- **Publisher.** Put in your publishing business name here.

Click *Save and Continue* to move to the next page.

KINDLE E-BOOK PRICING

- **KDP Select Enrollment.** Before you consider enrolling in KDP Select, read the *KDP Select—To Enroll or Not to Enroll* box below, and make your decision about KDP Select from there.

KDP Select—To Enroll or Not to Enroll?

The Pros

If you decide to enroll in KDP Select, you agree to make your book exclusive to the Kindle store for at least 90 days. Amazon sells 70% of books on the market. It favors books enrolled in KDP Select and will reward you by putting its vast marketing machinery behind your book, so your book becomes more visible.

All of a sudden, your book will appear in the features *Customers Who Bought This Item Also Bought This Book* and *Customers Who Viewed This Item Also Viewed.* If your book is not enrolled in KDP Select, your book will not appear in these features/recommendations on other Amazon pages.

Your e-book will also be included in Kindle Unlimited (KU). You can earn a share of the KDP Select Global Fund based on how many pages KU customers read of your book.

Enrolling in KDP Select also grants you access to a new set of promotional tools. It allows you to offer the book for free for five days or discount it for up to seven days using a Countdown Deal.

Why would you offer your book for free or at a discount? Because if it does well, your free book will rank in Amazon's Top 100 Free List and your discounted book will rank on Amazon's Top 100 Paid List. Once your book makes one of these lists, other readers are more likely to see it and download it. Not only will it improve its rankings in the sales ranks, which will lead to more readers and more sales, it will hopefully translate to much-needed reviews as well as sales once your book returns to its normal price. This is what is called a "loss leader strategy."

The Cons

For the time that your book is enrolled in KDP Select, you cannot make your e-book available in digital format on any other platform, including your own website.

My Opinion

Based on the successes of the authors I've assisted, I'd recommend enrolling in KDP Select as soon as you publish your books and take advantage of Amazon's vast marketing machinery. The benefits far outweigh the drawbacks.

However, this is a decision you must make yourself. I can't stop you from selling your e-book on your website, Apple iBooks, Kobo, Barnes & Noble, and any other platforms.

As it is only a 90-day commitment, you could test it by enrolling for 90 days before you decide to sell your e-book on IngramSpark or your website. If you are doing well, then keep going with this strategy. If not, simply cancel KDP Select after 90 days and publish your e-book on your website and IngramSpark.

❧ **Territories.** Select the territories for which you hold rights—select *Worldwide Rights* or *Individual Territories*. If you own the copyright on your book, click *Worldwide Rights*.

❧ **Pricing, Royalty, and Distribution.** There are two options to choose from—a 70% option and a 35% option.

Why, I can hear you ask, would anyone pick the 35% option when you can pick the 70% one? That's because there are conditions when choosing 70%. In a nutshell, to get the 70%:

1. You must price your book competitively between US\$2.99 and US\$9.99.

2. You must allow Amazon to sell your book in any territory for which you have rights (if you are a self-published author and you own the rights to your book, then that means the whole world).

3. The price must be the same or less than the price you are selling the e-book anywhere else (on your website, etc.).

What Should I Price My Kindle Book on KDP Amazon?

Pricing for your e-book will be different from your paperback and hardback versions. E-books are traditionally cheaper than their paperback and hardback counterparts. People expect to pay less for e-books because there are no printing costs.

I recommend doing some research on Amazon for books similar to yours. Have a look on online bookstores in the US, UK, Canada, and Australia, and price your book competitively with other books in your genre. For example, if most of the books in your niche are selling for US$3.99, then price yours at US$3.99. If many of them are US$0.99, then make yours US$0.99.

Don't forget you can change the price of your book at any time. So you should test different price points for your book even when you are selling well. I tested my book at US$0.99, US$1.99, US$2.99, and US$3.99 and found there was no difference in sales. However, when I raised it to US$4.99, sales dropped, so the perfect price point for my e-book was US$3.99.

The price of US$2.99 seems to keep the book from being devalued, while keeping it at a no-brainer investment for consumers.

It also depends on the type of book you have. See the next page.

TRADE BOOKS

These books contain a lot of content and are designed to teach readers about a particular subject. There may be a lot of books on the same subject, but they sell well anyway (for example, cookbooks and books on losing weight). Stick to the US$2.99–US$9.99 and 70% royalty for these e-books.

TEXTBOOKS

The more niche your book is, the higher the price you can charge for your book. A book on a particular type of software programming, for example, with its limited audience and limited competition, could potentially command a very high price of US$150–US$200. With those prices and no printing costs, the 35% royalty would be worth it.

LEAD GENERATION BOOKS OR REPORTS

These are short books or reports of around 20 pages and are usually priced between US$0.99 and US$2.99. The author's primary aim is to get readers to go to their website to buy the more expensive products or services that the author is selling. The book will usually have several calls to action inside it—inviting the reader to go to the author's website and get a free gift if they enter their email address. In this way, they now become part of the author's email database so the author can send out more content and hope the reader will eventually purchase more of their products.

FICTION

Novels seem to sell anywhere from US$0.99 to US$15.99 for better-known authors. If you are a first-time author, I'd advise keeping your prices at the lower end (between US$0.99 and US$2.99) to bring exposure to your books and build your readership. Then, once you've built a fan base, you can increase the price of your next book.

SETTING THE PRICE FOR ALL OTHER AMAZON SITES

Once you've entered your US price in the box, by ticking the boxes for Amazon India, UK, Germany, France, Spain, Italy, Japan, and Canada, they will automatically convert the US price using the exchange rate on the date you converted. You should make sure all your pricing ends in ".99" or ".95."

PUBLISH YOUR E-BOOK

By clicking *Save and Publish* at the bottom of the screen, you are confirming that you have all the necessary rights to make your book content available for marketing, distribution, and sale globally, and that you are agreeing to the KDP terms and conditions (read them if you need to).

TIME TO CELEBRATE!

Congratulations! You have completed the publishing process and will soon be a published Kindle author. You'll have to wait up to 72 hours until your book appears in the Amazon Kindle store. During this time, you won't be able to make any changes to your book, and it will say *In Review* next to your book on the KDP Bookshelf. As soon as your e-book is live, you can start your Amazon bestseller campaign to try to get to #1 in your three chosen categories. (See *Become a #1 Bestseller on Amazon* on page 272).

KDP E-BOOK PUBLISHING CHECKLIST

I have the KPF or ePub file and correct cover for KDP from my e-book converter: Yes ☐ No ☐

All my book details are complete on the KDP Bookshelf: Yes ☐ No ☐

I enabled Digital Rights Management (DRM):   Yes ☐ No ☐

I have previewed my e-book, and it reads well on Kindle devices or the Kindle app: Yes ☐ No ☐

I have enrolled my book in KDP Select: Yes ☐ No ☐

The pricing of my Kindle book is:

USD _____

GBP _____

EUR _____

CAD _____

AUD _____

I chose the 70% ☐ 30% ☐ royalty option.

Publish Your E-Book on IngramSpark

Please make sure you have read my previous section on the benefits of publishing your e-book exclusively on Kindle Direct Publishing before you decide to publish your e-book on IngramSpark.

IngramSpark will make your e-book version available across all major e-book distribution channels, including Apple and Barnes & Noble. Even though IngramSpark also offers your e-book version on Amazon as a Kindle version, I recommend publishing directly to Amazon Kindle Publishing to take advantage of the benefits of being directly on the KDP platform. That means that when you first sign up to IngramSpark, you'll need to opt out of the Amazon Kindle agreement by leaving the box unticked. You will be publishing your e-book directly to Kindle Direct Publishing after you publish your paperback. (See *Publish Your E-Book on Kindle Direct Publishing* in the previous section).

HOW TO PUBLISH YOUR E-BOOK ON INGRAMSPARK

The following steps assume that you already have a printed version on IngramSpark and that you have set up your account, tax information, and metadata for your printed book.

When you have your printed version available on IngramSpark, you're happy with it, and it is *Enabled for Distribution*, meaning live and available for sale, it's time to publish your e-book. To publish your e-book version on IngramSpark, you will need to do the following.

HAVE YOUR E-BOOK FILES BEFORE YOU START

Before you start it's a good idea to have the correct ePub files plus your front cover JPEG from your e-book converter. These have been created according to the IngramSpark submission guidelines (Please see page 195.)

LOG IN TO YOUR INGRAMSPARK ACCOUNT

Log in to your account at IngramSpark using your email and password.

SET UP YOUR E-BOOK

There is an option to *Convert to E-Book* from your paperback version. However, IngramSpark will take 15 days converting your paperback PDF to an e-book at $0.60 USD a page. If you have chosen to get your ePub files from an e-book converter, you will need to do the following instead.

Select *Upload a Title* on your Dashboard. Then select *E-Book Only*. IngramSpark will then ask you, "Do you have files ready to upload?" Click *No, But I Will Enter My Title Information and Submit Files Later*. To the next question, "What would you like to do?" please select *Distribute and Sell Book*.

COMPLETE ALL INFORMATION FOR YOUR BOOK

Add in all the information (metadata) as you did for the paperback and hardback versions, which includes the title, subtitle, the language in which the book is written, a short description, a long description, keywords, your imprint, categories, target audience, table of contents, and review quotes (see page 214). The easiest way to do this is to open a new tab on your browser, open the paperback version, and then copy and paste all the metadata from your paperback into your e-book version so they are exactly the same *except* for the ISBN, the pricing, and the files.

ISBN

Use a different ISBN for your e-book version. You can use the ISBN you set aside for your ePub in your list of ISBNs.

E-BOOK PRICING

The pricing for your e-book will be different from your paperback and hardback versions. Have a look at online bookstores in the US, UK, and Australia, take an average of 5–10 books in your genre, and price your book competitively with them. E-books traditionally cost less than their paperback and hardback counterparts. People expect to pay less for e-books because there are no printing costs. Make sure your Apple pricing ends in ".99" or Apple won't accept your e-book.

UPLOAD YOUR E-BOOK FILES

Upload your ePub and front cover files and submit. The e-book will take up to 15 days to show across all book retailers.

INGRAMSPARK E-BOOK PUBLISHING CHECKLIST

The ISBN for my IngramSpark ePub (e-book) version is:

_____

Pricing for your e-book:

USD _____

GBP _____

EUR _____

CAD _____

AUD _____

Congratulations, *you did it!*

You are now a PUBLISHED AUTHOR!

Self-Publishing Success Story—Amanda Hocking

Amanda Hocking, paranormal romance author and Kindle millionaire, demonstrated real strategic savvy when pricing her e-books on Kindle. She priced the first novels in her series at US$0.99 to make it a no brainer for her readers to buy and get them hooked on the story. The subsequent ones she made US$2.99—a price that was still easy to pay—but that also got her into the 70% royalty structure. After publishing her first novel on Kindle in April 2010, by the end of 2010, she had sold 164,000 copies, and in the month of January 2011 alone, she sold over 450,000 e-books (Pilkington 2012).

How are you going to celebrate?

_____

_____

_____

_____

_____

_____

_____

_____

Show Me the Money!

HOW DO I SEE MY BOOK SALES AND WHEN DO I GET PAID?

Here are the steps on how to access your royalties that you earn on IngramSpark and KDP.

INGRAMSPARK

1. Go to Ingramspark.com.

2. Type in your email address and password.

3. Click *Reports* and see your reports visually by clicking on *Sales, Titles, Compensation*, and *Transactions*. You can choose different time periods, including lifetime or this year.

4. IngramSpark will also provide a monthly sales report to you by email. These reports include the title, ISBN, quantity shipped, wholesale price of books sold, cost of printing, returns, and net compensation per title.

Payment: Royalties will be paid directly to your bank account. Payments are made to the publisher, via direct deposit or PayPal, 90 days from the end of the month in which the sales are reported.

KINDLE DIRECT PUBLISHING

1. Go to https://kdp.amazon.com/en_US/.

2. Type in your email address and password. You may receive a code to your mobile or email for security purposes. Enter the code.

3. Click on *Reports*. You can choose different time periods including lifetime, this year, this month, or last 90 days. Paperback books will only show on your Reports dashboard once they have been shipped.

Payment: These will be paid directly to your nominated bank account. KDP pays royalties every month, approximately 60 days after the end of the month in which they were earned. For example, you'll be paid in October for royalties earned in August, as long as they meet the minimum threshold.

8.

PROMOTE

"Writing a book without promoting it is like waving to someone in a dark room. You know what you have done but nobody else does."

—Madi Preda, author of *How to Promote and Market Your Book*

In this day and age, the biggest factor that determines the success of an author is how consistently they market and promote their book over time. While achieving the giant feat of publishing your book is worthy of applause, it's not yet time to put your feet up and watch the sales roll in. Popping the champagne is generally reserved for the actual book launch, and I can assure you, when done well, the marketing journey is one to be savored and enjoyed.

So, understand this from the get-go: your book won't sell itself!

It's very rare that this is the case, and you're much better off investing your resources in a well-planned marketing strategy than relying on this unlikely outcome. Most of the time, authors need to manage ongoing marketing activities and strategies, online and offline, to encourage sales. Comparatively speaking, publishing a book is 1% of a book's success. Marketing is the other 99%. If you can see this now as a marathon and not a sprint, you can manage realistic expectations about what's involved.

In my time as an independent publishing consultant, I've observed that the most successful authors actively and regularly engage with their market, whether that be an interview, talking at a library or creating new ad content. This is par for the course of living the life of a recognized author. So, let's claim it and embrace what's required when it comes to promoting and marketing your beautiful book. It deserves your support to flourish in the world, and you may even discover you enjoy it!

In this chapter, you'll learn how to promote your book. If an author tells me they haven't sold any books, my first question is: "What marketing have you done?" The answer is very often: "None."

Unfortunately, many writers bury their heads in the sand when it comes to marketing, yet they wonder why their books don't sell. It's the next logical step when sharing your book with the world—if you want to sell your book, you need to promote your book. If you commit to doing one marketing activity per day, you'll be well on your way to sales in a continuous and habitual fashion. Marketing practices will enhance your experience, not hinder it. So to get you started, here are my 14 most effective marketing tips guaranteed to boost your book sales.

1.
Create Your Author Platform and Start Building Your Audience Before Your Book Launch

Writing and publishing a book is a *huge* undertaking—I get it! It takes time, focus, and attention until it's done. So, if I mention that you need to have a website and social media platforms and start building an audience before you launch, you may start to feel like it's all too much. Then, you'll stop writing altogether! But please don't use this as a reason to procrastinate finishing your book. If it's too much for you at this time, then focus on finishing and publishing the book first. However, if you feel you can handle it, then use "downtime" while you're waiting for your book to be edited, laid out for print, and proofread to start creating your author platform.

An author platform means having a website and a presence on social media. Having an author platform shows that you're a serious author, and it will do a lot to raise your credibility. It's important to have these set up prior to launching your books, so you can sell your books directly to your target market from these platforms. Also, if you're going to be doing any media, the first thing journalists will do is look up your website to find out more about you.

Your website needs to be www.yourfirstnamesurname.com, not your publishing name—otherwise you'll attract people wanting you to publish their books! (See *Your Author Website Domain* on page 117 for more on this.) You are an author and need to be branding yourself as the author. Also, if you intend on having more than one book, you won't want to name the website the title of your book, as you'll end up having to have multiple websites, and this may become very difficult to manage. By having an author website, you'll get to keep all your books and services in one place.

Your author website can be simple. I recommend a five-page layout: a Home page, an About the Author page, an About the Book page, a Blog where you can post articles related to your book, and a Contact the Author page. You can get an inexpensive WordPress or Squarespace website done by a web developer on Upwork.com* or Airtasker.com.

If you'd like to handle the book orders yourself, you'll make more money by cutting out the middleman (i.e., other online distributors such as Amazon). However, you'll have to do the following tasks: get your web developer to accept payments to your website (PayPal or Stripe is good for this), get a quantity of books printed, package up the book nicely with a cover note, take the printed book down to the post office and mail it to the customer yourself. This is all fun for maybe a day but quickly becomes time consuming.

If you'd prefer *not* to deal with shipping out the books to customers, then once your book is live on Amazon KDP, give the KDP links to your web developer so that people can order directly from Amazon, and Amazon will take care of the printing and shipping on your behalf. Getting Amazon to fulfill your book orders will help your overall Amazon rankings.

Set up one or two social media platforms for reaching your target market. It's better to master one or two rather than do a bad job on several. Do this as soon as possible before you launch your book, because it takes time to build your audience on these platforms. Set up a public business page on Facebook, and name yourself as an author (for example, John Lee Author), so that it's different from your personal profile (John Lee).

Set up your Instagram and/or your TikTok profiles as an author. You can pay someone to set this up for you, or you can google *Facebook 101* or *TikTok 101* and learn the basics. Start practicing and learn how to post yourself.

You may not personally like Facebook, Instagram, or TikTok; however, you'd be crazy not to have a presence on these platforms. At the time of writing, there are 2.936 billion active Facebook users (Statistica 2024) and 1.452 billion active Instagram users (Data Reportal 2023) per month. TikTok is the fastest growing social media platform, with over 1.39 billion monthly active users (Singh 2024), and many authors are having great success with selling their books on this platform.

Once you set up your TikTok profile, start experimenting with posting short videos and using three to five hashtags, including #BookTok. BookTok is a subcommunity on TikTok focused on books and literature.

Once you have set up your Instagram profile and/or your Facebook profile and business page, start posting engaging, interesting, and inspirational memes, posts, articles, videos, and other relevant content about your subject. At this stage, the focus is on creating connections and building relationships. About a month before you launch, you can start to build excitement about your book so when you are ready to sell it, you'll have an audience eager to buy.

Make sure you post the content on your Facebook profile as well as your Facebook page, as the posts are more likely to be seen on your profile. (Facebook wants you to pay for ads on your business page these days.) If you have a nonfiction book, it's a really good idea to set up a Facebook group, too, so you can speak specifically to your audience about your subject and market your book as well as your other programs.

Please don't bombard people with trying to sell your book, as that can be a real turn-off. The ideal ratio is for 80% of your posts to give away useful content and 20% of your posts to promote your book. Post something every day using hashtags so you're tapping into the audiences following those hashtags. For example, *I'm excited to be planning the launch of my new book about homeopathy! #Homeopathy*

Consistency is key to building your audience over time.

Your website and social media platforms should have a unique author brand that oozes your brand personality (whether that be fun, authenticity, sophistication, warmth, etc.) and look consistent in their colors, font styles, photos, and messaging around the book.

I have set up a simple author website: Yes ☐ No ☐

I have a personal profile on Facebook: Yes ☐ No ☐

I have set up a public Facebook page as an author: Yes ☐ No ☐

I have set up a Facebook group: Yes ☐ No ☐

I have set up an Instagram profile: Yes ☐ No ☐

I have set up a TikTok profile: Yes ☐ No ☐

In the next 6–12 months, I will have:

Facebook friends (profile): _____

Facebook likes (page): _____

Facebook members (group): _____

Instagram followers: _____

TikTok followers: _____

2.
Make Your Book Available Online Before You Start Marketing It

All too often, I've seen authors start marketing their books without their books being available to purchase online. This is a *huge* mistake and can cost you numerous book sales. So make sure your book is live and for sale first.

Here's what I normally do: I publish the paperback and hardback on IngramSpark and order samples, but I don't click *Enable Global Distribution* and make the books live yet. I want the KDP paperback version to go live first.

Once I've seen and approved the IngramSpark samples, I order the KDP paperback version from my formatter and publish it on KDP. This goes live within 24–72 hours. As soon as it is live, I publish the e-book version on KDP. I make the e-book US$0.99, and I ask my Book Launch Review Team to purchase it and leave an honest review (See #3. *Become a #1 Bestseller on Amazon*).

At the same time, I click *Enable Global Distribution* on my IngramSpark paperback and hardback books. IngramSpark states that it can take between 1 and 15 days for your books to go live across all book retail platforms. Sometimes, the cover or other metadata is still not showing on retailers after 15 days. If this occurs, send an email to IngramSpark, and they will alert the particular bookstore.

While you are waiting for the IngramSpark versions to populate across all book retailers, focus your energy on promoting the live links of your KDP paperback and e-book. Remember, 70% of book sales will come from Amazon. Getting customers to purchase from these links keeps your Amazon rankings high, and you'll make better royalties per book from KDP than IngramSpark.

If you hover your mouse under *View on Amazon* on your e-book or paperback book on your KDP Dashboard, you'll see the direct links to your book in each Amazon store around the world. Please use these links to promote your books on social media and to your email list, so people can purchase your book from their own country's Amazon store. Otherwise, they may find if they reside in Australia and try to purchase your book from Amazon.co.uk, for example, they'll receive a message saying, "This title is not available."

If you have decided not to fulfill book orders yourself, then give your web developer the live links from KDP to put on your website. That way, when people go to your website and want to purchase your book, they'll be redirected to Amazon, and you won't have to worry about customer fulfillment.

My KDP paperback is live and available for purchase on Amazon:	Yes ☐ No ☐
My KDP e-book is live and available for purchase on Amazon:	Yes ☐ No ☐
My IngramSpark paperback and hardback are live and available for purchase:	Yes ☐ No ☐
I have given the live links to my web developer to put on my website so people can order the books from Amazon:	Yes ☐ No ☐

3.
Become a #1 Bestseller on Amazon

Now for the magic formula you've been waiting for! It is entirely possible to become a #1 Bestseller on Amazon in a particular category even if you are a first-time author. It is feasible to outrank the top-selling mainstream published authors because mainstream publishing companies do not optimize their books for Amazon. Becoming #1 on Amazon is less about selling thousands of books and more about learning how to play Amazon's algorithm game. But it will be huge for credibility and will do wonders for your career if you can put #1 Bestseller on Amazon in your book description, author bio, and other marketing materials.

Here is the system I have used to ensure that my clients become #1 in their categories once they publish:

1. First, the more specific the categories you choose, the better chance you have of reaching #1 in that category. So choose narrow categories over general ones when you publish your book. Amazon has recently updated its categories and some of them are now hidden, so it's best to use Publisher Rocket* to find the best categories and avoid the ones you can't become a bestseller in. Here's a link https://iinspiremedia--rocket. thrivecart.com/publisher-rocket/.

2. Second, help your rankings on Amazon by putting keywords in your title, subtitle, book description, and keywords. Publisher Rocket* can really help you find your best keywords.

3. Third, aim for a huge spike in sales on Amazon over a specified 48-hour period. Set your e-book at US$0.99 for the initial launch period so more people are inclined to buy. Amazon's algorithms will detect a lot of downloads of your book in this timeframe, and this will give you a good chance of hitting the bestseller list.

4. A few weeks prior to your launch date, start building your Book Launch Review Team. Email a list of 30–50 people you know and ask if they'd like to be part of your team. Tell them that this will entail reading an advanced reader copy (ARC) of your book, then purchasing the e-book for US$0.99 on Amazon on your specified launch date and leaving an honest review.

HOW TO FIND REVIEWERS FOR YOUR BOOK LAUNCH REVIEW TEAM

1. Start establishing your presence on Facebook and Instagram now so you have a community you can invite to be part of your launch team. This means making posts relevant to your niche, creating connections, and adding new friends and followers. Engage with people by asking for feedback on your cover and title, then later, ask people to join your launch team.

2. Start building an email list of people who are interested in your book, then invite them to be part of your team.

3. If you have a business, ask your clients. If you have a job, ask your peers and colleagues. If you belong to organizations, ask its members.

4. Join Facebook and LinkedIn groups relevant to your book topic, even while you are still writing your book. Become an active member of the group, and you'll find that they'll be a lot more willing to help you when it comes time to ask them to join your book launch team.

5. Join my Facebook group, *The Heart-Centred Author (Writing, Self-Publishing and Marketing Books)*. Start helping others with reviews, and they may return the favor when it's your turn.

6. If you are part of one of my paid programs, such as *The Authentic Author* or *Children's Book Empire* (see information on how to join at the back of the book), then you can ask the other members in the group.

Amazon has very strict review guidelines. They have banned compensated reviews (i.e., you are not allowed to pay someone or offer a free gift in exchange for a customer view). Nor does Amazon allow you to ask someone to purchase your book in exchange for a refund. They forbid asking someone specifically for a positive review, review swaps with other authors, and friends and family leaving customer reviews.

You *are* allowed to give a free advance review copy (ARC) of your book in exchange for an honest review. You *are* permitted to review the books of other authors whose book is in a different niche to yours, if you weren't part of their book publishing process (publisher, editor, contributor, etc.). You are also allowed to pay for reviews if you obtain them through independent review services such as Kirkus, Publisher's Weekly, and Readers' Favorite, and you can post these paid reviews under the "Editorial Reviews" section on your Amazon Author Central page.

So tell your reviewers that, if they enjoyed your book, you'd be most grateful if they would please leave an objective and honest customer review on your Amazon page on your specified launch date.

In order to leave a review on Amazon, the reviewer needs to have spent at least $50 on their country's Amazon site in the previous 12 months. Ask your reviewers in advance if they have done this. Otherwise, you may find that Amazon won't permit a number of your reviewers to leave you a review. Then, you'll need to find more reviewers.

A week or two prior to launch, email a PDF copy of your book to your launch team to give them time to read your book. Then as soon as your e-book is live for sale in the Amazon store, email the links to your e-book (you'll find these on your KDP Dashboard) to your email list, inviting them to purchase your e-book for US$0.99 and leave an honest review. This counts as a *Verified Review*. If they leave a review without purchasing your e-book, this counts as an *Unverified Review*, which is more likely to be removed by Amazon.

5. On your launch day, email your list, blog about your book, put the launch interviews on your websites and social media, do a Facebook live introducing the book, do an Instagram story about your book, and share your book on as many platforms as possible. Ask your friends, family, colleagues, book contributors, and your Book Launch Review Team to share it on social media too. You could even reach out to influencers who may happily share your book on social media with their friends and followers.

6. Try to get as many positive reviews as you can as quickly as possible, because the more positive reviews you have, the higher your book will rank on Amazon. Aim for a minimum of 10 five-star reviews on your Amazon page on the launch date. The more positive reviews, the more social proof that people liked your book, which in turn, leads to more sales. If you don't have reviews, potential customers will wonder why, and you'll sell fewer books. It's like going into an empty restaurant. It makes you wonder why you are the only one eating there!

WHERE YOU CAN FIND MORE REVIEWS

1. Run book promotions (see #5 on page 280).

2. You can get honest reviews from book review websites such as StoryOrigin, Booksprout, and HiddenGemsBooks, which are all sites to get book reviews from communities who are interested in reading and reviewing a book like yours.

3. Goodreads is a fabulous community for lovers of books, where members can track books they've read and post reviews for other readers. Create an author profile, join some groups, and join the R4R (Request for Reviews) boards. You can ask reviewers to post reviews to both Goodreads and Amazon.

4. Put a link in your email signature inviting reviews.

5. Put a request in the front or the back of your book requesting a review.

6. Email your list requesting reviews if they've read your book.

Please never buy reviews from websites like Fiverr.com* because Amazon may terminate your account.

7. Once you have reached #1 in your categories, take screenshots and share them on social media. Success builds on success. You can now include *Amazon #1 bestselling author* in your book descriptions and author bio on your website, and you can even ask your cover designer to put a gold badge on your cover if you feel so inclined!

8. Keep promoting your book hard, especially over the next 7–10 days, as you want Amazon to see regular sales, not just a once-off spike.

9. Start Book Promos (see #5) and set up a series of Amazon ads (see #6).

#GENIUS TIP!

My *Authentic Author* standalone course contains everything you need to know to write, publish, and launch a nonfiction book that gets to #1 on Amazon. This is an online course that you can do at your own pace and in your own time. It contains 40 lessons, and guest interviews with successful self-published authors. Here's the link to join: https://iinspiremedia.com.au/the-authentic-author-course/

I have asked 30–100 people to be part of my Book Launch Review Team to purchase my e-book and leave an honest review when I launch: Yes ☐ No ☐

I have signed up with a book review website such as Booksprout, StoryOrigin, or HiddenGemsBooks to get more reviews on Amazon: Yes ☐ No ☐

I have taken screenshots of my #1 rankings on Amazon and have shared these on social media: Yes ☐ No ☐

4.
Optimize Your Book on Amazon

Amazon is a brilliant, well-oiled marketing machine. If you've enrolled in KDP Select, Amazon will promote your book in *Hot New Releases* in each of your categories for 30 days—that's 30 days of hundreds if not thousands of new eyeballs on your book! Also, within a few weeks of publishing your book, you'll notice Amazon will start marketing your book to potential customers through *Frequently Bought Together, Products Related to This Item, Customers Who Bought This Item Also Bought,* and *Related Items Viewed by Customers.* This is a fabulous way for your books to be displayed for free to other customers in your niche.

If you want to get your book under *Customers Who Bought This Item Also Bought* quickly, ask your friends and family to purchase *your* book plus *another* book in the same genre. This way, your book will start getting paired alongside other books in its genre, and customers interested in that genre will begin buying it.

Join Amazon Author Central. This is an incredible opportunity to market yourself to your readers. Add your book, your author profile, and your professional bio photo and start blogging to your readers. You can even upload videos and book trailers to this page. You can get a fabulous, professional-looking book trailer done on Fiverr.com*. Here is the link: https://fvrr.co/2SxlAAV

Create A+ Content on your Amazon page. A+ Content allows you to add images, text, and comparison tables to your Amazon page to make your book stand out, engage readers, and give them more information as they consider buying your book. You can create A+ Content from the KDP Marketing page. From there, you'll go to the *A+ Content Manager* to layout, add images, and submit your content. Before you create A+ Content, please review the A+ Content Guidelines.

You can even join the Amazon Associates program to earn an additional 4% on each sale you create. Through Amazon Associates, you can produce custom links to your book, so when customers click these links and buy your book, you earn an extra 4% on each sale.

I have enrolled in KDP Select so my book will be advertised alongside others in my niche:	Yes ☐ No ☐
I have asked _____ people to buy my book as well as another book in my niche so my books will be shown as *Customers Who Bought This Item Also Bought*:	Yes ☐ No ☐
I have had a book trailer done on Fiverr.com*:	Yes ☐ No ☐
I have joined Amazon Author Central and set up my profile:	Yes ☐ No ☐
I have set up my A+ Content on my Amazon page:	Yes ☐ No ☐
I have joined the Amazon Associates program:	Yes ☐ No ☐

"It always seems impossible until it's done."

—Nelson Mandela, author of *The Long Walk to Freedom*

5.
Run Book Promotions

One of the benefits of enrolling into KDP Select for 90 days is that Amazon allows you to run Free Book Promotions and Kindle Countdown Deals. These are great ways to grow your audience and for new readers to find you. You can choose only one of these, not both, during a 90-day period.

FREE E-BOOK PROMOTION

You can offer your Kindle e-book for free for up to five days out of each 90-day KDP Select enrollment period. The five days don't need to be consecutive.

I'd encourage you to do these regularly to improve your Amazon rankings and gain new readers, new reviews, and new ratings. It also populates your *Also Bought* and *Related Items* sections, which gets your books paired alongside others in the genre, helping awareness and sales.

To schedule a Free Book Promotion:

1. Make sure your e-book is live, for sale, and enrolled in KDP Select.
2. Click on the *Marketing* tab.
3. Under *Run a Price Promotion*, choose *Free Book Promotion*.
4. Click *Create a Free Book Promotion*.
5. Click your book and then *Continue*.
6. Choose your start and end dates and click *Save Changes*.

KINDLE COUNTDOWN DEAL

A Kindle Countdown Deal is a great way to get more sales by temporarily promoting your book at a discount while still retaining your normal 70% royalty if your book is priced between US$2.99 and US$9.99. Amazon will show your original price and the discounted price, with a countdown timer to show how much time is left on the promotion. This creates a sense of urgency to buy your book before the price goes up again. For example, it may start at US$0.99, then go up to US$1.99, then US$2.99 over seven days.

Your e-book needs to have been enrolled in KDP Select for at least 30 days, and you can't have changed the price within the past 30 days prior to running the Countdown Deal. You can't run a Free Promotion and Kindle Countdown deal within the same 90-day period.

To schedule your Kindle Countdown Deal:

1. Make sure your e-book is live for sale and enrolled in KDP Select.

2. Click on the *Marketing* tab.

3. Under *Run a Price Promotion*, choose *Kindle Countdown Deals.*

4. Click *Create a Kindle Countdown Deal.*

5. Click your book and then *Continue.*

6. Choose your marketplace, date and time, number of Digital List Price increments, and starting Digital List Price. Click *Continue,* edit the table, then click *Add Promotion.*

BOOK PROMOS FOR YOUR E-BOOK

There are many e-book promotional sites like BookBub, Freebooksy, Bargain Booksy, BookRunes, the Fussy Librarian, Robin Reads, and many more. As soon as your e-book goes live, start booking in your promos. Scheduling your e-book to be featured on several of these sites can help you to drive sales of your book, find a new audience of readers, generate reviews, and improve your book's rankings. Some promos require a minimum of 5-10 reviews so book those as soon as your reviews start showing on Amazon.

My favorite is Freebooksy for a free e-book and Bargain Booksy for an e-book between US$0.99 and US$4.95. Neither of these require a minimum review count. Bargain Booksy ranges from US$18–US$250 for a promotion. Make sure your e-book is priced at the discounted price all day until midnight of the promotion date. Otherwise they won't run it, even though you've paid for it.

I also love the Written Word Media 1-day, 3-day or 5-day promo stacks. These do varying combinations of Freebooksy, Bargain Booksy, The Fussy Librarian, Facebook and Amazon ads to large audiences and range from US$45 - $580 depending on the genre.

Getting a BookBub Featured Deal is one of the best investments you can make as an author. Your e-book will be emailed to *hundreds of thousands* of readers, and this site is considered the best for number of downloads, which will skyrocket your rankings, but it costs between US$100–US$4,000 to book, and the wait list is huge. Keep trying if you don't get accepted the first time.

I have booked the following book promotions:

_____

_____

_____

_____

_____

_____

6.
Use Amazon KDP Ads to Build Exposure and Sell Books on Amazon

Running ads for your KDP books can help you reach new customers. You can target customers using keywords, including similar author names and titles to yours, to show your ads on search and detail pages on Amazon. With Amazon advertising, you can create custom ads for readers who are already searching for books like yours on Amazon. You set the daily budget you want to spend and the maximum amount you're willing to pay when customers click your ad. Ads are run on a cost-per-click, auction-based model. The more competitive your cost-per-click bid is, the more likely your ad will be displayed. I recommend you set bids at the maximum amount you are willing to pay for a click on your ad. You'll never be charged more per click than what you bid. To get a really good overview of how ads work, I recommend doing Dave Chesson's free Amazon Marketing Services (AMS) course here: https://iinspiremedia--rocket.thrivecart.com/publisher-rocket/5da9eae7a2e46/

HOW TO DO KDP ADS

1. Go to your Amazon KDP Bookshelf.

2. Choose the live KDP book you want to advertise.

3. Click *Promote and Advertise* under *Kindle e-book* or *Paperback*.

4. Select a marketplace for advertising from the dropdown menu and click *Create an Ad Campaign*. Amazon.com is the largest marketplace in the world, followed by Amazon.co.uk. You can run ads on Amazon.com (US), Amazon.ca (Canada), Amazon.co.uk (UK), Amazon.de (Germany), Amazon.es (Spain), Amazon.fr (France), Amazon.it (Italy), and/or Amazon.com.au (Australia) if you choose.

If you haven't set up an *Amazon Advertising* account for this marketplace, sign in with your existing KDP credentials to register. Repeat this step for each new marketplace in which you wish to advertise.

5. Choose an ad type: *Sponsored Products* or *Lockscreen Ads*. *Sponsored Products* ads promote your title to readers as they search for books. *Lockscreen* ads reach customers on their devices when they are reading. I recommend only choosing *Sponsored Products*.

6. You select your products to advertise and choose keywords or product attributes to target, or you may let Amazon's systems target relevant keywords automatically. You control how much you want to spend on your bids and budgets and can measure your ad performance. I recommend using Publisher Rocket* to find relevant keywords to use in your ads. It makes the process far easier and quicker than doing it yourself. Here is the link: https://iinspiremedia--rocket.thrivecart.com/publisher-rocket/.

7. Submit your ad for review. It takes up to 72 hours to be approved. The ads will be rejected if they contain unsubstantiated claims, personal pronouns ("your" and "you"), swear words, grammatical errors, and/or inappropriate images. For a full list of guidelines, see here: https://advertising.amazon.com/resources/ad-policy/creative-acceptance.

8. It's important to tweak the ads every few days rather than take a set-it-and-forget approach to ensure you are paying only for keywords that convert to book sales or Kindle Unlimited downloads. Otherwise, you may find your credit card is being regularly charged for keywords that are clicked on but aren't converting.

9. Set a start and end date for the campaign (three months is a good timeframe). Otherwise, it's easy to forget a continuously running ad and you may end up with bill shock.

7.
Use Joint Ventures

This is one of my favorite marketing tips, as I've seen many authors sell a lot of books via this strategy. While you're in the process of writing, ask yourself, "Who else has my target readers?" Think about organizations with big email databases with whom you could partner to sell your books. Approach them with a compelling offer to split the royalties 50/50 or 60/40 if they are willing to promote your book to their large networks. For example, a book about internet dating sold 3,000 copies via the internet dating website RSVP in its first week! Another example is when author Lisa Messenger published her book *Happiness Is*, she did a joint venture with Clinique, who gave away a copy of her book when people bought the perfume Happy. She was able to move so many more books that way.

What organizations have my target market and may be interested in doing a joint venture with me?

_____

_____

_____

_____

_____

_____

_____

_____

_____

8.
Create a Physical Book Launch

Giving your audience and the media an actual physical place, date, and time for your book launch will create momentum and buzz around your book. You may well want a book launch with family and friends to celebrate the hard work you've put into this book, and you should do that if you want to! You deserve it. It is likely to end up being one of the happiest events of your life as you celebrate the fulfillment of your dream of becoming a published author with your loved ones.

But hiring an expensive venue and doing an evening event is not a strategic marketing move, as it is likely to counteract any profits you make on your book, and media don't tend to come out in the evening after work. Unless of course you invite key people in your industry who will then invite you for speaking or work opportunities in the future.

If you want to get strategic about your launch, then first ask yourself—*where do my target audience hang out?* Then piggyback on the back of an existing event to ensure you have a ready-made audience. For example, if your book is aimed at parents of deaf children, host the event at a parents' day at a school for deaf children.

If you'd like the media to turn up, make sure you have your launch during the day—preferably a Tuesday, Wednesday, or Thursday between 11 a.m. and noon. Then pack the hour with amazing content, including you as the author speaking about the book and/or other contributors of the book who share their personal stories or expert opinions. Can you invite other speakers or a celebrity who would complement your launch and speak about some of the topics or themes in the book?

I'd encourage you to learn how to contact the media yourself. Create a list of media contacts, contact them directly with your news, and build a relationship with them. If you don't wish to do this, then hire a media and PR expert; however, most PR agents will put you on a three-month retainer to allow them to get some media traction, and this can amount to thousands of dollars each month.

To do your own media and PR, make a list of all the media you'd like to have attend, then call them and let them know about your launch about two to three weeks prior to the date. Pitch your event in one or two compelling sentences (date, time, opportunities for photos, footage of people sharing their stories, themes discussed, etc.). You can find their contact details by googling the email address and phone number of each media outlet you want to contact, or you can buy a media list. The media will usually ask you to email through a media release. See *How to Write a Media Release for a Book Launch* on the next page.

Follow up with another phone call in a few days to ensure that they have received it and that your event is in their diary. Their editorial team will make a decision on the actual morning of your launch as to whether or not they will attend, depending on other events of the day.

Remember, it's not necessarily the book launch that will attract the media, but more, it's *the story behind the story.* The hot topics in the media at the moment are issues like domestic violence, depression, mental health issues, and bullying, to name a few. The media may not find the launch of a children's book newsworthy, but what about if the author suffered prostate cancer, which led him to write children's books in the first place? The media could then interview the author about his cancer battle and his reason for writing children's books, get some of the latest stats on how many men are likely to be diagnosed with prostate cancer each year, interview an oncologist, take some footage of the author's grandchildren, and then you've got an inspiring news piece! For more on this, see the *Media Release* that led to my client being featured on the evening news below.

Make sure you have your printed books available at least two weeks prior to the date of your launch. Otherwise, due to unforeseen delays, you may end up with no books to sell at your launch.

Also, be sure to invest in a *tap and go* for book purchases. You can buy a Square from places like Officeworks for A$60, which turns your smart phone into an EFTPOS machine. You can then take it wherever you go to sell books (library talks, conferences, when someone asks you for a copy of your book, etc.).

Finally, make sure your paperback, hardback, and e-book are available for sale online. Otherwise, you will miss out on vital book sales when your story hits the media!

HOW TO WRITE A MEDIA RELEASE FOR A BOOK LAUNCH

A media release is a one-page document containing all the vital pieces of information to spread the word about your book to the media.

Here's one of my media releases that ended up getting my client on the evening news as well as in newspapers, magazines, and podcasts.

MEDIA RELEASE—For immediate release—May 5, 20XX

LOU'S LEGACY

When grandfather of six, Lou Silluzio, was diagnosed with prostate cancer, he decided the only way out of his depression was to leave a legacy by creating a book for each of his six grandchildren.

Lou will be sharing his courageous, inspiring story and reading his children's books to the students of **St. Mary Immaculate Primary School in Ivanhoe this Thursday, May 7, from 11 a.m. to noon.**

Prostate cancer affects 1 in 11 Australian men and is most common in men over 65. Prostate cancer can be treated in a variety of ways, including surgery, radiotherapy, and hormone therapy, all of which Lou has undergone.

Each of Lou's books has a moral and teaches children important values. His first book, *Milana and the Escalator*, tells the story of three-year-old Milana, who learns a valuable lesson about safety after running away from her grandfather.

Lou Silluzio, author, says, "My grandchildren are the inspiration for my books. I wanted to leave a legacy for them by creating a personalized book for each of them."

The book has so far been very well-received by family and friends. Amanda Truda, mom of Rafael, almost three years old, said, "My son loved *Milana and the Escalator*! Hopefully he now stops running off at every opportunity."

The Principal of St. Mary Immaculate Primary School, Kerry Willcox-McGinnes, said, "We were delighted to be part of such an inspiring event. The children love the books!"

Lou is donating 10% of the book's profits to the Epworth Medical Foundation.

For more information on Lou's story and books, please see www.lousilluzio.com. Lou's books are available for purchase in all Australian bookstores. To request an interview, please call *[number]* or email *[email]*.

A media release should contain the following:

1. A strong headline to grab the reader's attention.
2. The date and the city.

3. On the top right of the release, say *For immediate release* if you don't mind journalists doing stories about it in the lead up to the launch or *Embargoed until [date]* if you want stories to go out on the date of the launch.

4. The who, what, where, when, and why of your launch are in the first paragraph so it's a quick read for journalists.

5. Images of the book and the author, or even a video of the author talking about the book and why it's important.

6. Quotes from your target market and quotes from experts.

7. Details about what opportunities journalists will get during the launch—interviews with the author, contributors, and experts—and photo or footage opportunities on the day.

8. Facts, figures, and stats about the niche—for example, stats on prostate cancer.

9. Contact information and where to contact you to learn more, including website, email address, and phone number.

10. Where people can buy your book—your website and URLs for your books.

The Power of a Virtual Book Launch

Thanks to technology, the way we host book launches has completely evolved! What used to be crowded public gatherings requiring hefty budgets and sometimes lofty guest lists have now transformed to DIY rock your own virtual book launches over Zoom (or other platforms). You can still energize your audience and create the celebratory live event your book deserves from a distance and with far greater reach.

An online launch will give you the opportunity to engage with a global audience, which is exactly what you need to widely promote your book. You can record the event, invite more people than may be possible in a physical space, and significantly save on costs using virtual technology.

People find that virtual book launches are wonderful experiences, cherished long after the book is introduced. They capture poignant moments and insightful discussions along with a formal-yet-fun shared recognition of the journey the author has taken to this point in birthing a beautiful book to the world.

My physical/virtual book launch will be held on: _____

at: _____

from: _____

I have created a media release to send out to my media list: Yes ☐ No ☐

Where would I like to get media mentions? Which TV or radio shows, newspapers, and magazines?

_____

_____

_____

My media contact list:

_____

_____

_____

_____

9.
Build Your Email List

Email is the most effective and inexpensive way to connect with your readers, and build an ongoing relationship with them. With an email list, you can promote and share new ideas, your current and future books, and other products and services, as well as direct your readers to where they can purchase them—whether that be a link to your website or an online bookstore like Amazon or Barnes & Noble.

- Start collecting email addresses by offering something of value in return for an email address.

- In your social media accounts or in your email signature, give away a free chapter of your book, a free e-book, or free e-course on your website in exchange for people's email addresses.

- Advertising a free webinar on social media can also grow your email list exponentially.

- All your blog posts on your website should encourage people to sign up for a free chapter, e-book, or course so you continue to grow your list.

Use an email marketing program like Mailchimp, MailerLite, or ActiveCampaign to email your list. Communicate with your list every month by sending them an e-newsletter with facts or news related to you, your books, or promotions related to your upcoming books and services.

I have started an email list: Yes ☐   No ☐

I have a free giveaway/lead magnet on my website   Yes ☐   No ☐
to collect email addresses and grow my website:

I have connected email marketing software such as   Yes ☐   No ☐
Mailchimp to my website so I can email my list:

In the next 6–12 months, my email list will have _____
email contacts.

10.
Readings and Book Signings

Most physical bookstores have an account with IngramSpark so they can order your books at the 40%–55% wholesale discount for your book on IngramSpark. However, you will still need to alert them that your book is available.

With smaller, independent bookstores, you'll have to approach them with your newly published book and negotiate directly to stock your book. Most expect a 40% RRP discount.

Go to the bookstore and introduce yourself to the store manager. Show them a copy of your beautifully published, high-quality book. Tell them you are just about to launch the book and will be doing a lot of marketing of the book over the coming months. Then ask if they would like to stock a few books in their shop. Say you'd be interested in doing an in-store book signing and reading in the next few weeks. Ask them if they would be interested. Mention you'll do a copromotion on social media and your website to let people know you'll be there. This is a win-win for both you and the bookstore, as you will be bringing in more potential customers.

#GENIUS TIP!

Most libraries have a budget for talks and workshops (around A$350–A$400 per author talk in Australia). Approach individual libraries directly, tell them that you are an author and have just published a new book. Offer to do a one-hour author talk or a workshop depending on the content of your book. Bring copies of your book to sell at the event.

Where else can you do talks? Rotary clubs, business networking hubs, and clubs and associations are all looking for speakers to speak at their next events. Contact as many as you can. Ask them if they have a speaking budget. If they don't, offer to speak for free. You never know where your next book sale or opportunity will come from. Sign up with a speakers' bureau. Be available to share your message with as many audiences as you can. Speaking can have a huge impact on book sales.

What readings and book signings do you want to do?

_____

_____

_____

_____

_____

_____

_____

The Power of Influencers and How to Approach Them

Influencer marketing is a savvy tool worth including in your marketing strategy. Imagine someone with a broader platform than you who decides to showcase and talk up your book and/ or product. The ripple effect reach of an influencer is hugely impactful and can tremendously boost your sales or even jumpstart your author career.

Approach influencers in a thoughtful manner, using tact and a little background research to increase your chances of them noticing you. The trick is to get them to read your email among the many emails they receive.

Once you've established a connection with them by publicly supporting their work and engaging with them on social media, follow these tips on how to stand out in their inbox:

1. Craft a personalized email that is succinct and simple.

2. Refer to their content in your request and draw a connection between your work and theirs.

3. Be straightforward with your request—if you want them to dedicate a blog about your book or do a review of a product, then specify this.

4. Explain your value—claim what you believe you can contribute to the audience.

5. Follow their recommended channels of contact.

6. If you don't succeed at first, continue building the relationship. You never know what opportunities may emerge.

Here is an example email to get you started:

Hey [first name],

I've been a huge fan of your work, in particular [insert content], and felt compelled to reach out to you about it.

After sharing your blog on [insert topic] and noticing how many people it resonated with, I wondered if you also knew about [insert topic], which inspired a new book I launched earlier this year.

I'd love for you to take a look at my blog post about it and consider mentioning the book on your social media platform. I think you'll find we have an audience with many shared interests.

Let me know what you think!

Best,
Your name

11.
Approach Websites, Blogs, and Podcasts and Become Active in Facebook Groups in Your Genre

Tim Ferris's first book *The 4-Hour Workweek* hit #1 on the *New York Times* Bestseller list and stayed there for three months with no book launch, no media or PR, and no book signings! What he did was approach all the blogs in his niche, and he created content that would appeal to their interests, not his. He asked interested bloggers to post his story and read his book. He built relationships with the bloggers and maintained them. The bloggers posted his content because it was interesting to their readers. They read the book, loved it, and raved about it on their blogs. The rest is history.

Do a Google search on the top 10 websites/blogs and podcasts in your genre. Introduce yourself and your book to their owners and offer to do an article, guest post, or interview that would be of interest to their readers.

Use the Power of Facebook Groups

There are tens of millions of Facebook groups, and 1.8 billion people use Facebook groups—they are a gold mine to find your target readers. Join groups that are specific to your niche. For example, if you have a parenting self-help book, then go to the Facebook search bar to find and join *Parenting Groups* that look appealing to you. Become active in these groups—be helpful, comment, answer questions—and soon, people will start to notice you. Some groups do not allow promotion, so check the rules before you post, or risk being banned. Some Facebook groups allow you to promote on certain days so take advantage of these days regularly.

I have approached 10 websites in my niche:　　　Yes ☐　No ☐

The websites I've approached are:

1. _____

2. _____

3. _____

4. _____

5. _____

6. _____

7. _____

8. _____

9. _____

10. _____

I have approached 10 podcasts in my niche: Yes ☐ No ☐

The podcasts I've approached are:

1. _____

2. _____

3. _____

4. _____

5. _____

6. _____

7. _____

8. _____

9. _____

10. _____

I have joined 10 Facebook groups in my niche: Yes ☐ No ☐

The Facebook groups I've joined are:

1. _____

2. _____

3. _____

4. _____

5. _____

6. _____

7. _____

8. _____

9. _____

10. _____

12.
Use Facebook Ads to Spread the Word

Many authors use Facebook ads to successfully reach their target market, and it can be an effective strategy so long as you are earning more than you spend.

Facebook has over 2.9 billion active users who check their account multiple times per day. With information available about each user, you have the ability to set up highly targeted ads to your specific audience and get a lot of exposure and potentially sales for your book.

HOW DO YOU CREATE A FACEBOOK AD?

- Set up a Facebook business page as your author profile (e.g., John Elliot Author) to differentiate from your personal profile (John Elliot). You cannot do ads from your personal profile.

- Use the Facebook ads manager to create your ad and select your target audience, readers who would have an interest in a book like yours. You can select countries, age groups, gender, and interests.

- You can choose different ad objectives, such as boosting your Facebook posts, promoting your Facebook page, sending people to your author website, sending people directly to your Amazon page, getting people to claim your free offer, or getting video views.

- Experiment with different ads with different messages, different spend amounts (between US$10 and US$20 each) and different links (such as your author website or a direct link to Amazon) and see which ads convert to book sales. You can track the metrics in Facebook ads manager to see which ads work and which don't.

- ❧ It's important to set a start and end date for the campaign. Otherwise, you may end up with a huge bill on your credit card, as it's easy to forget a continuously running ad.

- ❧ Facebook will reject your ad if it has too much text in it. If you are using your book cover as the image, it may be a good idea to get your graphic designer to remove some of the text from your book cover, as Facebook includes the text on the cover in your text count.

13.
It's *Not All* About the Book, but It Is *All* About the Book!

I often say this to my students and clients. I say, "It's all about the book", because the book—and by book, I mean the *printed* book (not just an e-book)—is what gives you the credibility, the authority, and the leverage. It opens doors to a wealth of opportunities that may not otherwise have come your way without having the book. Opportunities may include speaking to the media; writing articles on your subject; commanding coaching and consulting fees; creating courses, workshops, and high-end programs; speaking at events; collaborating with other influencers in your field; and traveling to other states and countries promoting your book.

But I also say, "It's not all about the book!" because too many people falsely believe they are going to sell thousands, if not millions, of books and can then give up their day jobs and retire. This is simply not the case. I've seen authors make a full-time income from their books, but they've worked incredibly hard to make this happen through having multiple books (not just one) available for sale on book retail platforms and consistently marketing them over time.

So, think carefully about what you want to create as a result of and in conjunction with your book. Would you like to become a coach, mentor, or consultant in this area? Would you like to create workshops, courses, seminars, or retreats?

The cost of a book can range from US$0.99 (Kindle version) on Amazon to US$49 for your hardback. What other products can you offer to your target market that are perhaps the same value as your book but are in a much higher price bracket?

An audio program or a downloadable product costing US$97? One-on-one consulting at an hourly rate (say US$100–US$300 an hour)? A workshop, course or weekend retreat costing US$297? Or a larger program costing US$2,997?

Don't forget to mention these in your books, and let people know how they can contact you, as well as offering them in your emails to your subscriber list.

I have a grander vision beyond the book: Yes ☐ No ☐

I'm going to do one-on-one or group mentoring, coaching, or consulting: Yes ☐ No ☐

I'm going to present workshops/seminars: Yes ☐ No ☐

I'm going to run a retreat: Yes ☐ No ☐

I'm going to create a downloadable audio or video product: Yes ☐ No ☐

I'm going to create a course or program: Yes ☐ No ☐

I'm going to create a downloadable audio or video product: Yes ☐ No ☐

My Big Picture Vision
(i.e., what I am going to offer to my target audience)
Be as specific as possible.

_____

_____

_____

_____

_____

_____

_____

_____

_____

_____

14.
Never Stop Marketing!

Marketing is an ongoing pursuit, so try to do one marketing action every day or every few days. Bestselling authors aren't created overnight. Many authors have said it took them a minimum of 18 months to become a bestseller. It's taken some authors many years for one of their books to become a bestseller, and then all the previous books are subsequently purchased by their fans.

Approach magazines, websites, newsletters, and organizations that have your target market as readers. Write an engaging article that can be published in a newsletter, magazine, or blog. Be active in Facebook groups and do a free giveaway of your books. Offer to do interviews on podcasts and YouTube. Offer to speak at events, libraries, and rotary clubs.

As Jack Canfield, coauthor of the Chicken Soup for the Soul series, said: "Never, never, give up!" After first being rejected by 144 different publishers, he now holds the Guinness World Record for having seven books simultaneously on the *New York Times* Bestseller list.

Being an author is a marathon, not a sprint. It is about committing to the journey and enjoying every minute of all the surprises and adventures along the way.

Self-Publishing Success Story—James Redfield

James Redfield wrote *The Celestine Prophecy* in 1992 and printed 1,500 copies himself. The book is about synchronicity, so he traveled all over the country giving it to the first person he saw in every bookstore. The book soon became a word-of-mouth sensation, and it wasn't long before Warner Books contacted James. He had an informal phone auction with two mainstream publishers and eventually sold the rights to Warner for the highest advance. The book became a *New York Times* Bestseller and went on to sell more than 20 million copies worldwide; it has been translated into 34 languages and was turned into a movie in 2006 (Redfield 2020).

It's rare to see a city embrace its style heritage with as much respect as Tokyo. A traditional kimono captured on a busy street corner of Shibuya.

What on earth

BEAUTY FOOD   MARIA AHLGREN

india mahdavi   Home Chic   Flammarion

9.

CELEBRATE

Since publishing your book, it's important to keep a record of what you've achieved and how your life has changed. Writing it down reminds you what new doors have opened, what opportunities have come your way, and how you have grown as a person.

1. _____

2. _____

3. _____

4. _____

5. _____

6. _____

7. _____

8. _____

9. _____

10. _____

How are you going to celebrate these successes? A nice bottle of wine or champagne? A meal out with family or friends? Treating yourself to a massage or a weekend away? Buying yourself something new to wear or a new item for the house?

1. _____

2. _____

3. _____

4. _____

5. _____

6. _____

Writing and publishing a book and becoming an author is one of the most joyous and rewarding experiences in one's life, right up there with giving birth to a baby. I wish you so much joy and love on this wondrous journey.

Julie xo

12 Month Planner

This Month

Top Priorities

1.

2.

3.

What I Need to Do to Make This Happen

1.

2.

3.

Insights and Learnings

1.

2.

3.

Challenges

1.

2.

3.

Wins

1.

2.

3.

12 Month Planner

This Month

_____

Top Priorities

1. _____

2. _____

3. _____

What I Need to Do to Make This Happen

1. _____

2. _____

3. _____

Insights and Learnings

1. _____

2. _____

3. _____

Challenges

1. _____

2. _____

3. _____

Wins

1. _____

2. _____

3. _____

12 Month Planner

This Month

_____

Top Priorities

1. _____

2. _____

3. _____

What I Need to Do to Make This Happen

1. _____

2. _____

3. _____

Insights and Learnings

1. _____

2. _____

3. _____

Challenges

1. _____

2. _____

3. _____

Wins

1. _____

2. _____

3. _____

12 Month Planner

This Month
_____

Top Priorities

1. _____

2. _____

3. _____

What I Need to Do to Make This Happen

1. _____

2. _____

3. _____

Insights and Learnings

1. _____

2. _____

3. _____

Challenges

1. _____

2. _____

3. _____

Wins

1. _____

2. _____

3. _____

12 Month Planner

This Month

_____

Top Priorities

1. _____

2. _____

3. _____

What I Need to Do to Make This Happen

1. _____

2. _____

3. _____

Insights and Learnings

1. _____

2. _____

3. _____

Challenges

1. _____

2. _____

3. _____

Wins

1. _____

2. _____

3. _____

12 Month Planner

This Month

_____

Top Priorities

1. _____

2. _____

3. _____

What I Need to Do to Make This Happen

1. _____

2. _____

3. _____

Insights and Learnings

1. _____

2. _____

3. _____

Challenges

1. _____

2. _____

3. _____

Wins

1. _____

2. _____

3. _____

12 Month Planner

This Month
_____

Top Priorities

1. _____

2. _____

3. _____

What I Need to Do to Make This Happen

1. _____

2. _____

3. _____

Insights and Learnings

1. _____

2. _____

3. _____

Challenges

1. _____

2. _____

3. _____

Wins

1. _____

2. _____

3. _____

12 Month Planner

This Month
_____

Top Priorities

1. _____

2. _____

3. _____

What I Need to Do to Make This Happen

1. _____

2. _____

3. _____

Insights and Learnings

1. _____

2. _____

3. _____

Challenges

1. _____

2. _____

3. _____

Wins

1. _____

2. _____

3. _____

12 Month Planner

This Month
_____

Top Priorities

1. _____

2. _____

3. _____

What I Need to Do to Make This Happen

1. _____

2. _____

3. _____

Insights and Learnings

1. _____

2. _____

3. _____

Challenges

1. _____

2. _____

3. _____

Wins

1. _____

2. _____

3. _____

12 Month Planner

This Month
_____

Top Priorities

1. _____

2. _____

3. _____

What I Need to Do to Make This Happen

1. _____

2. _____

3. _____

Insights and Learnings

1. _____

2. _____

3. _____

Challenges

1. _____

2. _____

3. _____

Wins

1. _____

2. _____

3. _____

12 Month Planner

This Month

_____

Top Priorities

1. _____

2. _____

3. _____

What I Need to Do to Make This Happen

1. _____

2. _____

3. _____

Insights and Learnings

1. _____

2. _____

3. _____

Challenges

1. _____

2. _____

3. _____

Wins

1. _____

2. _____

3. _____

12 Month Planner

This Month
_____

Top Priorities

1. _____

2. _____

3. _____

What I Need to Do to Make This Happen

1. _____

2. _____

3. _____

Insights and Learnings

1. _____

2. _____

3. _____

Challenges

1. _____

2. _____

3. _____

Wins

1. _____

2. _____

3. _____

Notes and Reflections

Glossary

ASIN: Amazon Standard Identification Number

ASIN stands for *Amazon Standard Identification Number* and is a 10-character unique identifier assigned by Amazon.com to identify your book on Amazon. When you publish your e-book on Kindle Direct Publishing, you don't need an ISBN; Amazon KDP will give your e-book version an ASIN.

EPUB: E-Publication

EPUB stands for *e-publication*. It is an open e-book standard file format that is optimized for viewing on devices. It is compatible with many e-reading devices and apps because the file automatically resizes to fit the size of your screen. It is the recommended format to publish your e-book on IngramSpark.

HTML: Hypertext Markup Language

HTML stands for *Hypertext Markup Language*, a coding language used for web pages. If you apply some basic HTML to your book description on KDP, it will create paragraph spaces, bold, and italics on your page to make your book description look more visually appealing. Without it, your book description will just be a block of text.

ISBN: International Standard Book Number

An ISBN is an International Standard Book Number. ISBNs were 10 digits in length up to the end of December 2006, but since January 1, 2007, they now always consist of 13 digits. Every version of your book (hardback, paperback, and ePub) requires a separate ISBN. Also, if you publish your paperback version on two different platforms, such as IngramSpark and KDP, you will need separate ISBNs.

JPEG: Joint Photographic Experts Group

JPEG stands for *Joint Photographic Experts Group* and is a popular image file format. The term refers to a type of compression that makes these image files much smaller than the RAW files that are taken by high-end digital cameras. Your cover designer and/or formatter will prefer to see your images or illustrations as 300dpi JPEGs for your book.

KDP: Kindle Direct Publishing

KDP stands for *Kindle Direct Publishing* and is a publishing platform owned by Amazon that allows you to publish both e-books and paperback books for free.

KDP Select

KDP Select is a free Kindle book program run by Amazon that gives you the opportunity to reach more readers and earn more money at no additional cost. If you are enrolled in KDP, your book will be enrolled in the KU program so readers can download your e-book and you will be paid for pages read of your book!

KPF file

KPF stands for Kindle Package Format. Amazon recommends uploading an ebook in KPF format to fit all Kindle devices and avoid any formatting issues.

KU: Kindle Unlimited

KU stands for *Kindle Unlimited*, an Amazon subscription service that allows customers to download as many e-books and audiobooks as they want, choosing from over 1 million titles. Subscribers pay US$11.99 a month and can cancel anytime. If your e-book is enrolled in KDP Select, your e-book will be enrolled in KU, and you will be paid for pages read of your book.

PDF: Portable Document Format

PDF stands for *Portable Document Format* and is a file used to publish print books. Once your book has been laid out, it gets converted to PDF to preserve the layout of the pages. PDFs are not reflowable, so their text size cannot be adjusted for display on various devices.

References

Alter, Alexander and Elizabeth A. Harris. "What Snoop Dogg's Success Says About the Book Industry." *The New York Times*, April 28, 2021. https://www.nytimes.com/2021/04/18/books/book-sales-publishing-pandemic-coronavirus.html.

Booktopia. "Rachel Bermingham & Kim McCosker." Accessed December 15, 2020. https://www.booktopia.com.au/rachael-bermingham-kim-mccosker/author21.html.

Bowman, Cynthia. "How Much Is Amazon Worth?" Go Banking Rates, August 4, 2023. https://www.gobankingrates.com/money/business/how-much-is-amazon-worth/.

Coker, Mark. "Why Jamie McQuire Returned to Self-Publishing." Smashwords, February 26, 2015. https://blog.smashwords.com/2015/02/why-jamie-mcguire returned-to-self.html.

Condie, Ally. *Matched*. London: Penguin, 2011.

Culleton, Tracy. "Odds of Being Published." Fiction Writer's Mentor. Accessed September 29, 2021. http://www.fiction-writers-mentor.com/odds-of-being-published/.

Doran-Myers, Miranda. "73% of Adult Readers Prefer Printed Books, According to Gallup Survey." Library Research Service, January 18, 2017. https://www.lrs.org/2017/01/18/73-of-adult-readers-prefer-print-books-according-to-gallup-survey/.

Duffield-Thomas, Denise. *Chill and Prosper: The New Way to Grow Your Business, Make Millions, and Change the World*. Carlsbad, CA: Hay House, 2022.

Errera, Rob. "Printed Books vs eBooks Statistics, Trends and Facts [2024]." May 31, 2023. https://www.tonerbuzz.com/blog/paper-books-vs-ebooks-statistics/.

Ferriss, Tim. "How Does a Bestseller Happen? A Case Study in Hitting #1 on the New York Times." *The Tim Ferris Show* (blog), August 6, 2007.

https://tim.blog/2007/08/06/how-does-a-bestseller-happen-a-case-study-in-hitting-1-on-the-new-york-times/.

Fleck, Anna. "Amazon Dominates Book Sales Almost Everywhere." Published April 23, 2024. https://www.statista.com/chart/28042/share-of-respondents-who-bought-books-from-amazon/.

Ford, Arielle. *Wabi Sabi Love: The Ancient Art of Finding Perfect Love in Imperfect Relationships.* San Fransisco: HarperOne, 2012.

Genova, Lisa. "Self-Publish or Perish!" LisaGenova.com (blog), Accessed April 16, 2021. https://www.lisagenova.com/single-post/2008/08/06/self-publish-or-perish.

Golden, Arthur. *Memoirs of a Geisha.* London: Vintage, 1998.

Goleman, Daniel. *Emotional Intelligence.* 10th ed. New York: Bantam Books, 2007.

Higginbotham-Hogue, Nicole. "Pinning Demographics in the Writer's Market." *NewsBreak Original*, November 15, 2021. https://original.newsbreak.com/@nicole-higginbotham-hogue-1590928/2434841844952-pinning-demographics-in-the-writer-s-market.

Hughes, Donald L. "The Shack: Self-Published to 15 Million Copies Sold." *Christian Writing Today*. Accessed June 12, 2021. https://christianwritingtoday.com/the-shack-self-published-to-15-million-copies-sold/.

Klems, Brian A. "How Hugh Howey Turned His Self-Published Story 'Wool' Into a Success (& a Book Deal)." *Writer's Digest*, January 23, 2014. https://www.writersdigest.com/be-inspired/how-hugh-howey-turned-his-self-published-story-wool-into-a-success-a-book-deal.

Leong, Melissa. "How and Why I Self-Published." *National Post*, December 7, 2012. https://nationalpost.com/entertainment/books/how-and-why-i-self-published.

Leslie, Mark. "Episode 13—Going Your Own Way with T. S. Paul." *Stark Reflections*, March 23, 2018. https://starkreflections.ca/2018/03/23/episode-13-going-your-own-way-with-t-s-paul/.

McGaw, Graeme. "Rachel Abbott's Books in Order." Book Series in Order. Accessed June 11, 2021. https://www.bookseriesinorder.com/rachel-abbott/.

Pilkington, Ed. "Amanda Hocking, The Writer Who Made Millions by Self-Publishing Online." *The Guardian*, January 12, 2012. https://www.theguardian.com/books/2012/jan/12/amanda-hocking-self-publishing.

Redfield, James. "The History of the Celestine Series." Celestine Vision. Accessed August 5, 2021. https://www.celestinevision.com/the-history-of-the-celestine-series/.

Ridley, R. W. *The Takers: Book One of the Oz Chronicles*. Charleston, SC: BookSurge, 2005.

Sagan, Carl. *Cosmos: The Story of Cosmic Evolution, Science and Civilisation.* Los Angeles: Abacus, 1983.

Sandler, Lauren. "Because This Public Defender is Also a PEN Award-Winning Novelist." *New York Magazine*, December 13, 2013. https://nymag.com/news/articles/reasonstoloveny/2013/public-defender-sergio-de-la-pava/.

Savitz, Eric. J. "After Facebook's Surge, There Are Now 5 Tech Stocks Worth at Least $1 Trillion." *Barron's*, June 29, 2021. https://www.barrons.com/articles/facebook-tech-stocks-worth-at-least-1-trillion-51624922591.

Shea, Lisa. "Acknowledgements Page Layout." Accessed October 22, 2021. https://lisashea.com/lisabase/writing/gettingyourbookpublished/partsofabook/acknowledgements.html.

Stranger, Tracey. *How to Overcome Stress Naturally: Take Control of Your Mental & Emotional Life.* Brisbane: Global Publishing Group, 2022.

Talbot, D. "Odds of Getting Published Statistics." *Wordsrated*, February 2, 2023. https://wordsrated.com/odds-of-getting-published-statistics/.

TTBOOK. "Author Discusses How 'The Martian' Went from Blog to

Blockbuster." *Wisconsin Public Radio*, October 6, 2015. https://www.wpr.org/author-discusses-how-martian-went-blog-blockbuster.

Vaheesan, Sandeep and Tara Pincock. 2024. "Throwing the Book at Amazon's Monopoly Hold on Publishing." *The Nation*, Published January 8, 2024. https://www.thenation.com/article/economy/throwing-the-book-at-amazons-monopoly-hold-on-publishing/.

Recommended Reading

Cameron, Julia. *The Artists Way: A Spiritual Path to Higher Creativity.* Chicago: Souvenir Press, 2020.

Gundi, Gabrielle. *Kindle Bestseller Publishing: Publish a Bestseller in 30 Days!* Kindle Direct Publishing, 2019.

Penn, Joanna. *The Creative Penn Podcast: Writing, Publishing, Book Marketing, Making a Living with Your Writing* (podcast). https://www.thecreativepenn.com/podcasts/.

Poynter, Dan. *Dan Poynter's Self-Publishing Manual: How to Write, Print and Sell Your Own Book.* Para Publishing, 2007.

Platt, Sean M. and Johnny Truant. *Write. Publish. Repeat.: The No-Luck-Required Guide to Self-Publishing Success Paperback.* Sterling & Stone, 2015.

Recommended Resources

Creativity support	*The Artist's Way* by Julia Cameron

Find a ghostwriter or editor

Upwork*	https://upwork.pxf.io/c/347458/1062918/13634

Get a writing accountability coach

iinspire media	iinspiremedia.com.au

Do some research on books in your genre

Amazon	amazon.com
Publisher Rocket*	https://iinspiremedia--rocket.thrivecart.com/publisher-rocket/

Register your publishing name

Australia	https://asic.gov.au/for-business/registering-a-business-name/
US	https://www.sba.gov/business-guide/launch-your-business/choose-your-business-name
Canada	https://www.canada.ca/en/services/business/start.html
UK	https://www.gov.uk/set-up-sole-trader

Get a publishing logo	Fiverr*	https://fvrr.co/2SxlAAV

Get your ISBNs

Australia	https://www.myidentifiers.com.au/identify-protect-your-book/isbn/buy-isbn
US	https://www.myidentifiers.com/identify-protect-your-book/isbn/buy-isbn
Canada	https://library-archives.canada.ca/eng
UK	https://www.nielsenisbnstore.com/Home/Isbn

Get a barcode free or on donation

Bookow	https://bookow.com/resources.php

Get a professional cover design

99designs*	https://99designs.qvig.net/c/347458/177079/3172
Fiverr*	https://fvrr.co/2SxlAAV

Get your standard book size

IngramSpark	http://www.ingramspark.com/plan-your-book/print/trim-sizes
KDP	https://kdp.amazon.com/en_US/help/topic/G201834180

Find an illustrator

Fiverr*	https://fvrr.co/2SxlAAV
99designs*	https://99designs.qvig.net/c/347458/177079/3172

Book layout and typesetting

Upwork	https://upwork.pxf.io/c/347458/1062918/13634
99designs*	https://99designs.qvig.net/c/347458/177079/3172
iinspire media	iinspiremedia.com.au
Fiverr*	https://fvrr.co/2SxlAAV

Publish your book	IngramSpark	ingramspark.com
	KDP	https://kdp.amazon.com/en_US/
Get publishing help	iinspire media	iinspiremedia.com.au

Get an e-book converter

Upwork	https://upwork.pxf.io/c/347458/1062918/13634
iinspire media	iinspiremedia.com.au

Get a website domain name	GoDaddy	godaddy.com

Market your book

Amazon Ads	https://advertising.amazon.com/
Free course with Dave Chesson	https://iinspiremedia--rocket.thrivecart.com/publisher-rocket/
Publisher Rocket*	https://iinspiremedia--rocket.thrivecart.com/publisher-rocket/
Rocket Tutorials	https://iinspiremedia--rocket.thrivecart.com/publisher-rocket/5e8f51fc1dd46/

Acknowledgments

Thank you to my brilliant beta readers—Kate Olivieri, Peta Webb, Cinthia Del Grosso, Virginia Warren, Annie Grimwade, Isabella Valassidis, and Stephen Marantelli. Your feedback was invaluable in shaping both the workbook and the journal into what they have become.

Thank you to Charlotte Claire of CC Copy for your wordsmith services in helping create additions to this book that made it flow so beautifully.

Thank you to Cortni Merritt (of SRD Editing Services) who copyedited this book according to the *US Chicago Manual of Style*, 17th edition. It was a joy to work with you.

Thank you to Sophie White for the typesetting and layout of my book. Your expertise has been invaluable.

Thank you to my wonderful Mum and Dad, Gill and Dave Postance, my brother Gregg, and my sister Hayley for your ongoing love, support, and encouragement.

Thank you to my fabulous circle of friends for your never-ending love and support.

Thank you to my incredible clients and students who have made the world a better place with your books.

To my twin boys Ollie and Arie, who are the joy of my life and have allowed me to believe in miracles.

Would You Like to Work with Julie?

Julie offers one-on-one coaching/mentoring as well as group programs so you will achieve your goal of writing and publishing your book.

The Children's Book Empire Program

This is a three-month immersion into writing, publishing, and launching your very own children's book. This is a combination one-on-one and group program with Julie and a small number of participants, as well as 10 guest speakers. It is run online twice a year. For more on this program, please see https://iinspiremedia.com.au/childrens-book-empire/.

The Authentic Author Program

This is a three-month immersion into writing, publishing, and launching your very own nonfiction book. This is a combination one-on-one and group program with Julie and a small number of participants, as well as 10 guest speakers. It is run online once a year. For more on this program, please see https://iinspiremedia.com.au/the-authentic-author/.

The Authentic Author Course

This is an online course that you can do at your own pace and in your own time. My Authentic Author course contains everything you need to know to write, publish, and launch a nonfiction book that gets to #1 on Amazon. It contains 40 lessons, and recorded guest interviews with successful self-published authors. Here's the link to join: https://iinspiremedia.com.au/the-authentic-author-course/.

Private One-on-One Coaching

Julie has a very limited number of spots available for one-on-one coaching and only takes on a small number of clients at any given time. If you'd like to work with Julie to get your book out into the world, please email her at info@iinspiremedia.com.au (iinspire with two ii's), tell her what you would like to achieve, and she will get back to you within a week.

Contact Julie Postance

Independent publishing consultant

I INSPIRE
MEDIA

info@iinspiremedia.com.au

iinspiremedia.com.au

facebook.com/JuliePostanceWritePublishandPromoteYourBook

facebook.com/The Heart-Centred Author (Writing, Self-Publishing and Marketing Books)

instagram.com/writepublishandpromoteyourbook

linkedin.com/in/JuliePostancePublishing

If you enjoyed this book…

If you enjoyed this book and received helpful tips and actionable strategies from it, please consider letting others know. Here are some ways you can do so:

- Please share your thoughts in a review on Amazon. Your feedback is extremely helpful—both for other readers to decide whether this book will be useful for them and for authors to get the word out about their book.

- Please leave a review on Goodreads.

- Tell your friends about this book on your blog, podcast, or YouTube channel.

- Share it on Facebook, Instagram, X, Threads, TikTok, Pinterest, or LinkedIn.

- Mention this book to your friends, family members, and colleagues at work.

Your support is greatly appreciated. Thank you for taking the time!

www.ingramcontent.com/pod-product-compliance
Lightning Source LLC
Chambersburg PA
CBHW041255040426
42334CB00028BA/3019